The Divorce Surgery

The art of untying the knot

Samantha Woodham and **Harry Gates**

Thorsons

All efforts have been made to ensure that the information set out in this book is accurate and reflects the laws of England and Wales as at 13 January 2022. It should be used to supplement rather than replace professional legal advice.

Thorsons
An imprint of HarperCollins*Publishers*
1 London Bridge Street
London SE1 9GF

www.harpercollins.co.uk

HarperCollins*Publishers*
1st Floor, Watermarque Building, Ringsend Road
Dublin 4, Ireland

First published by Thorsons 2022

1 3 5 7 9 10 8 6 4 2

The Parenting Plan at the end of Step 5 is a product owned and designed by the Children and Family Court Advisory and Support Service (Cafcass). We thank them for allowing us to display an abridged version of it in this book.

A catalogue record of this book is available from the British Library

ISBN 978-0-00-850551-6

Printed and bound in the UK using 100% renewable electricity at CPI Group (UK) Ltd

MIX
Paper from
responsible sources
FSC
www.fsc.org
FSC™ C007454

This book is produced from independently certified FSC™ paper to ensure responsible forest management.

For more information visit: www.harpercollins.co.uk/green

For the 42%, their friends and their family

Contents

Prologue:
Golden Rules

If you are separating, or contemplating divorce, it can feel as though the weight of the world is on your shoulders. But know this: it's going to be OK. In fact, it's going to be better than OK, and sooner than you think.

In this book we'll take you through everything we know about divorce, cutting out the jargon, and simplifying it into a 10-Step Divorce Plan, so you can not only survive divorce, but thrive.

Before we begin, here are some golden rules which are fundamental to the way we view divorce and encourage you to see it too.

Divorce is *not* a failure

The fact that your marriage is ending is a life change, pure and simple. You are both evolving in ways which do not involve sharing the same bathroom for the next four decades. As a society, we still attach so much stigma to divorce. Just say the word and the associations are all grim: guilt, conflict, shame, expense. But 42 per cent of marriages end in divorce.[1] Which means you are certainly not alone. It is a product of the fact that we are all living a really long time, far longer than was ever imagined when the construct of marriage was created, centuries ago. If you were told, in your late twenties, that you would be in the same job for the next 60 years, or the same house, or the same style of clothes, it would sound ludicrous, because it is. It is just as ridiculous to suggest that, at the same age, you will be able to identify a romantic relationship which will last a lifetime. All you can do is make the right choice at the time, with respect and love. And when it comes to ending the marriage, you can and should do it in the same way.

A 50-year marriage is not the 'gold standard'

We are all programmed to believe the 'success' of a marriage should be measured by its length. Get to 60 years and you will even receive a telegram from the queen. But a 50-year marriage is not the 'gold standard'. Again, this is a myth. You may have friends who seem as blissfully happy now as they were when they married decades ago. If so, that is great for them. They have evolved as human beings in ways which complement each other. But that's just luck. And it doesn't mean they are going to have a happier life than you. They may never have the opportunity to truly redefine themselves, to love again, differently, or to embrace the adventure that comes when you success-fully navigate a life change like divorce. They are perfectly entitled to their happiness, but you are perfectly entitled to yours. Your life will be first rate, not second best.

You do not have bad judgement

We speak to separating and divorcing couples on a daily basis. Whenever we can, we use this phrase. And it never loses its power. So here we go again: Your decision to get married was *not* a mistake. It does *not* mean you have bad judgement or that you are destined to have relationships which end. It was the right decision at the time. Unless you are extremely unlucky, you will have made many happy memories along the way. The fact that it is now time for a change is not an indictment of your judgement. Don't let the ending contami-nate everything that went before. You will learn a lot about yourself from this experience, and about what you want from life in the years ahead. You will find joy again. Don't doubt yourself.

Divorce itself doesn't harm children; a bad divorce, and a bad marriage, do

Children, above all, do best when they can just focus on being children. We'll talk about this at much greater length later in the book, but research consistently shows that what causes children emotional harm is not divorce *per se*, but prolonged and entrenched conflict between their parents. This can happen within a bad marriage, just as it can within a bad divorce. Don't let it. If you are married but arguing all the time and making each other miserable, don't delude yourselves into thinking that your children are unaware. Seek external, impartial and professional support. Keep any toxicity, as far as you can, out of your children's home. And don't stay in an unhappy marriage 'for the sake of the children'. Please don't. They will do so much better seeing their parents thriving apart than suffering together. Remember, you are modelling for your children. Would you want them to stay in an unhappy relationship or would you want them to find a way to move apart with kindness and dignity?

You aren't breaking up your family, you are reshaping it

The term 'broken family' is hugely outdated and, to put it simply, wrong. If you have children, you will be co-parents for life. And save for those tragic, abusive situations, your fellow co-parent can be a long-term source of support. Not just for your children, but for you too. Nobody else will be more receptive to a call at 3 a.m. when your youngest is running a fever. Be extremely careful, when you are navigating divorce, to protect and nurture the co-parenting relationship you share. This is an opportunity to reshape your family unit. You are still a family, and will always be a family, just in a different form. Also, when we talk about family, please know that this is meant for everyone. You are a family unit whether you have children or not.

You don't need a lawyer on speed-dial

The irony that we are lawyers telling you this isn't lost on us. But it is true. Every separating couple needs legal advice, because these are huge decisions to take concerning family and finances. But don't be fooled into thinking lawyers have all the skills you need. We don't. A divorce is about so much more than the legal process. It is a redefining moment in your life and you need impartial emotional support so you can make the long-term decisions that are right for you and your family. Counsellors and divorce coaches can help you become 'emotionally ready'. The only reason to rush to legal advice is if you feel your safety is at risk, or if there are serious issues about one partner hiding assets, or jurisdictional complexities. But these scenarios only affect a very small minority of couples, thankfully.

We believe that when it comes to divorce, 'it takes a village'. Yes, you need good, impartial legal advice. But you also need financial expertise, co-parenting tips and emotional support. So, don't let the legal part take so much time, money and headspace that there are no reserves left for anything else. And when the time comes to choose a lawyer, choose wisely. Ensure they share your values. Be wary of hourly rates; fixed fees are available. And if you both want to share a lawyer and split the costs, you can.

Prioritize emotional support

Life is short. None of us are happy all the time, and the Instagram view of the world can be extremely unhelpful in that regard. But in all the thousands of divorcing spouses we have met, no one has ever said they are divorcing 'on a whim'. A divorce will be the product of months, often years, of soul-searching. You may feel blindsided by the divorce. You may feel relieved, even joyous. You may feel grief-stricken. You may be riddled with guilt. You may be all these things, and at some stage you probably will be. We aren't therapists, but in our experience as lawyers, the most common barrier to a successful divorce is not understanding how to process the emotional response. So, recognize that you need to navigate these emotions, ideally together. We'll speak later in much more depth about emotional support, but the main point is: please access it, and do so as early as possible. Have the hard conversations in a safe space, away from home, with a professional helping you both. Let the emotions out. Conduct the post-mortem. Rediscover your empathy for each other and start to build a different relationship.

Divorce may not be your choice, but the way you divorce can be

We all like to be in control. One of the hardest parts of any relation-ship breakdown can be coming to terms with the fact that someone else's choice has been imposed upon you. Please try not to look at it like that. A happy relationship relies on the happiness of two people to make it work. Your own personal happiness does not.

If you are mourning the loss of your relationship, get emotional support to help you process your feelings. Also, take heart. New adventures are coming. And in the meantime, respect yourself and the marriage you had by ending it well. Conflict causes emotional harm. Choose not to hurt yourself.

It is easier to divorce badly than to divorce well

So much easier. It is natural to focus on what *you* want, what *you* need, rather than what you *both*, in separate households, will need. But remember that the only way to divorce well, and to reach an agreement which is fair, is for you to consider each other's needs as well as your own.

Some people talk about divorce as entering a deep, dark forest. It is an analogy we understand but would never use. The way we see it, divorce is a fresh start. It is emerging from a dark forest into a sunnier upland. And that is the image we want you to keep in mind. Because there are going to be big bumps in the road. You are disentangling yourself from a long-term intimate relationship. It won't be a smooth process. But when you hit that first bump, if you've been told to expect a forest, then a forest is what you'll get – your confirmation bias will inevitably lead you to think, 'Oh, here I am in the forest. Horrid, dark and no clear way through. Just as I feared.' But if you're expecting to emerge from a forest, your mind will help you. You will think, 'Yup, forest, I see you, but the sunnier uplands are out there and I'm going to keep on this path until I get there.'

Beware of your 'support network'

Your family and friends can make all the difference when it comes to divorcing well. So much so that we have given them their own step in this book. But beware, they can be as much of a hindrance as a help. What you need from your friends and family is emotional support, love and distraction. What you don't need is ex-bashing.

Remember that your close friends and family will also need to process this life change. They will have their own feelings of sadness. But don't let them dictate your narrative. They might think they are supporting you by spending drunken evenings describing in detail why your ex was awful, and never right for you. But you will find at the end of the evening you feel worse, not better. If you are working hard to keep positive and reject the 'failure' narrative, you need to get your friends and family on the same page. We started The Divorce Surgery to give separating couples access to joint impartial advice from a single lawyer they shared. But as the business has grown and evolved, we've realized that we do more than that: we give separating couples permission to be decent to each other, and we give them a narrative to tell their family and friends and the parents at the school gates: 'There's really no drama. We're actually sharing a lawyer. We're working this out together.'

Abuse is *never* OK

This book is for couples who want to navigate divorce well – and together. If you are in a relationship where you don't feel safe, for whatever reason, please immediately seek the help of a family law solicitor. The Family Court has many powers it can and will use to protect you and any children.

The 10-Step Divorce Plan

We have created a 10-Step Divorce Plan which takes you through all the stages you need to navigate. It is the product of what we've learned from all the divorcing couples we've worked with.

Here it is:

STEP 1
SETTING OUR GOALS

STEP 2
AGREEING OUR PLAN OF ACTION

STEP 3
DECIDING WHAT PROFESSIONAL SUPPORT WE NEED

STEP 4
MAKING SHORT-TERM PLANS

STEP 5
STARTING TO TALK ABOUT THE CHILDREN

STEP 6
BUILDING OUR FINANCIAL PICTURE

STEP 7
REACHING A CO-PARENTING AGREEMENT

STEP 8
REACHING A FINANCIAL AGREEMENT

STEP 9
MANAGING OUR FRIENDS AND FAMILY

STEP 10
MAKING OUR RESHAPED FAMILY A LIFELONG REALITY

But feel free to jump around – the order isn't prescriptive. And the plan works at any stage of the process, from contemplating separation to being in the throes of divorce litigation. Go to whichever step happens to speak to you, and we'll navigate you gently through the process from there.

Let's get started.

STEP 1

||||||||||||||||||||||||||||||||||||||||||||||||||||||||||||||||||||||||||||||||

SETTING OUR GOALS

||||||||||||||||||||||||||||||||||||||||||||||||||||||||||||||||||||||||||||||||

'How do we start this right?'

The first step is all about framing the narrative for your divorce and setting your goals.

FRAMING THE NARRATIVE

The story of your divorce is crucial. It will impact how you approach every aspect of our 10-Step Divorce Plan. The way you tell your friends, family and colleagues that you are getting divorced will dictate how they will view this life change you are about to embark upon, and what kind of support they will provide. It will also frame how you view yourself.

There's nothing intrinsically bad about divorce

That sounds so counter-intuitive, doesn't it? And shows how programmed we all are to view divorce as something unappealing and to be avoided. Can you imagine listing divorce as a life goal? And yet we'll accept other life transitions without this heavy overlay of emotional stigma.

So the first thing to know is that your mindset will be warped and you'll need to question your own instinctive reactions to divorce and what it means, as well as those that the outside world will impose upon you.

We call this negative conditioning the 'divorce lens'. Let's look at other significant life changes you may have made, but through the divorce lens.

Decided you want to move from the city to the country?

> *'Ooooh, how exciting! Can I come to stay?'*

vs divorce lens:

> *'But you committed to the city at the age of 23 and I never thought you were the kind of person at age 45 who would abandon those urban ideals.'*

Moving jobs?

> *'Oh, wow, that sounds like a great career move!'*

vs divorce lens:

> *'But how has that made your employer feel? I know absolutely nothing about your employment relationship or what you do day to day, but from my position of complete ignorance on these issues I really feel you should try a bit harder and hold out in this job that's making you deeply unhappy.'*

Similarly, everyone will have an opinion, often ill-founded, on your marriage, and your divorce. So the first thing you both need to do is buttress yourselves against the in-built and often deeply unhelpful reactions of those around you. And know that they are wrong. You will set the narrative.

Why get married anyway?

To start at the very beginning, why do any of us get married in the first place? If you do an internet search with that question, you'll get a ream of academic studies about why marriage is good: you'll live longer, you'll earn more money, your children will live longer, you'll be less depressed, more loved and have more sex (yes, apparently); and just as many studies about why marriage is bad: you'll have weaker relationships with your friends and family, be less politically engaged and more isolated.

Or, take these two quotes:

Marriage responds to the universal fear that a lonely person might call out only to find no one there. It offers the hope of companionship and understanding and assurance that while both still live there will be someone to care for the other.

Justice Anthony Kennedy, a former associate justice of the Supreme Court of the United States, his majority opinion in *Obergefell v Hodges*

vs

If you're afraid of loneliness, don't marry.

Chekhov

But who sits down and makes a pros and cons list when contemplating a marriage proposal? For the vast majority of couples, it's an instinct. A study in 2013 found[1] that 88 per cent of the general public surveyed gave the top reason for getting married as love.

So, what is love?

If we marry for love, all things being equal, shouldn't we stay married for love? But most of us would admit that love is something well beyond our control. There is some scientific research[2] to tell us that, at its core, love is the result of a basic evolutionary mechanism that emerged millennia ago, enabling us to focus our attentions on one partner to aid procreation and the stability of the family unit.

Love can be shown on brain scans, in particular as activity in the ventral tegmental area, a region of the brain which makes the stimulant dopamine and sends it to other areas. So, at a biological level, love is a function of brain chemistry, which is changing all the time. Both falling in love and falling out of love are functions of our subconscious.

This is important for your narrative as a divorcing couple. You didn't choose to fall out of love. And you can't force yourself to love again. Acknowledging that relieves you both of a significant burden.

And what is life all about?

I assure you we'll get back to the practicalities of divorce soon, but these gargantuan life questions matter when you're aiming to approach divorce with the right mindset.

At the heart of our life experience is the pursuit of happiness. But, in the same way that we can't control love, happiness can be elusive. As Benjamin Franklin said:

> *The [US] Constitution only gives people the right to pursue happiness.*
> *You have to catch it yourself.*

As a society, we live in an individualistic age. We are far less likely than our grandparents to stay in situations that make us uncomfortable or unhappy. Fortunately, we are more tolerant of divorce in general (although there is still a great deal of progress to be made) and we are more inclined to weigh the temporary unhappiness of a divorce against the permanent horrors of staying put. As Joan Rivers put it, 'Half of all marriages end in divorce – and then there are the really unhappy ones.' In 1960, as we stood on the cusp of a revolution in social freedom, there were fewer than 24,000 divorces in England and Wales. In 2019 there were 108,000, a fourfold increase, despite the fact that the number of marriages had fallen by a third in the same period[3] (the law was changed to make divorce easier in 1971, contributing to the increased pace of divorce throughout the Seventies and Eighties). Joan would be encouraged.

Basically, we are less inclined to settle for 'good enough' when 'perfect' is just out there, waiting for us if only we're bold enough to grab it. Compromise can be seen as something of a dirty word across all walks of life – in politics, in art, in business, and of course in personal relationships. And it is true that you can compromise too much. You may already both be exhausted by the daily micro-concessions your marriage has required of you, from the food you eat, to the TV you watch, to the friends you see, to the Christmas Day routine you have endured 'even though everyone knows that's not the way you do it', all the way through to the much bigger issues, such as the career you 'sacrificed' to bring up your children or from the long hours you 'endured' in a job you hated because the bills needed paying.

One rationale for marriage which has always resonated with people is that you get married because you are happier together than apart. Of course, none of us is happy every day. Life is full of both light and shade. But when the unhappy days heavily outweigh the happy ones, it is right to reflect on why. We set out on a journey to make ourselves and each other happy. But over time, for some couples, this becomes impossible. Their relationship, once a source of great joy, becomes the root of their unhappiness.

There is no one to blame

Approached in this way, that it is the relationship that has failed, not the individuals, forms the backbone to a blame-free divorce.

There will be potential (and highly attractive) scapegoats all around you: long working hours, an affair, emotional disengagement, undesirable friends, hostile extended family members, financial mismanagement. Don't fall down those rabbit holes. These are symptoms, not causes.

If your happiness and your former partner's happiness are now mutually exclusive, you have a problem which neither of you can overcome. All you can pursue is your own happiness. If that road causes the other to be unhappy, don't force them to travel with you. Equally, you cannot spend your precious time on this planet making someone else happy without regard to your own needs.

'So why are we getting divorced?'

Big, expansive ideas about the pursuit of happiness are fine, but for many couples that doesn't quite cut it. They need a more specific narrative. Why, when it was so great at the start, is it so bad now? Was it even that good at the start, or was this divorce a seed there from the get-go, just waiting to emerge at the most inopportune time?

It is so difficult to remember emotions. When you look at photos, you can see the smiling faces, and no doubt remember the great meal or the funny anecdote that brought forth those smiles. But can you remember how you felt then? Probably not. Why? Well, largely because you are a different person now.

Our personalities were long thought to be fixed by the time we reached our thirties, but the latest research suggests they continue to change throughout our lives.[4] Our traits are ever shifting, and by the time we're in our seventies and eighties we've undergone a significant transformation. 'The conclusion is exactly this: that we are not the

same person for the whole of our life,' says René Mõttus, a psychologist from the University of Edinburgh.[5] Psychologists call the process
of change that occurs as we age 'personality maturation'. It's a gradual,
imperceptible change that begins in our teenage years and continues
into at least our eighth decade on the planet.

So, 'growing apart' is precisely that. You were probably extremely
compatible when you met and fell in love. But you've both changed.
And now you aren't any more. You may well have said and done
unkind things to each other as you fought against the personality
mismatch that developed. Why is the person who used to make you
so happy now making you so sad? But if you can stand back and
acknowledge that you're both facing this same (seemingly) unresolv-
able dilemma, you'll soon realize the solution is staring you both in
the face. You need to free each other from this relationship that was
meeting your needs but isn't any more. And that isn't anyone's fault.
You're just different people now. And you both deserve to be happy.

You can't control love. You can't make somebody else happy. That's
OK. That's life.

'WHAT IS OUR DIVORCE STORY?'

Your divorce story is going to become a narrative which you fall back
on when times get tough. So it's important to take some time before
you commit to that narrative, even to yourself. Whether you were the
one to instigate the divorce conversation or not, you need to invest
time in rationalizing in your own mind what has happened, and why,
before you let the world in.

A case study example:

MARY AND GEOFF

Mary and Geoff were married for 37 years. When they first met both were working professionals on track for good careers. Geoff's career took him all over the world. He had some successes, but the gruelling hours meant he was rarely at home during the working week. So the family commitments fell squarely on Mary's shoulders. After the birth of their first child, she gave up work, and at the time was happy to do so. She could see that the combined demands of their jobs were incompatible with the all-consuming nature of caring for young children. Something had to give. And whilst she had at times enjoyed her career, she had also found it stressful. She was still relatively junior. A baby felt like a greater life purpose she was happy to pursue.

Fast-forward 30 years. The children are grown, independent and happy (on the whole). Geoff is still working as hard as ever. Mary's life is full and largely independent of her husband's. One Saturday morning Geoff leaves his mobile on the kitchen table whilst having a shower. He hasn't selected the privacy settings on WhatsApp, meaning that when messages arrive they flash up on the screen. Which is how Mary discovers Geoff's affair with Fiona, a work colleague who is 30 years younger than Geoff (and in fact younger than their youngest child).

There is so much to unpack about Mary and Geoff, and we will return to their story at various stages in the book. But focusing now just on their divorce story, Mary has been completely blindsided and she has a ready-made narrative: she is the wronged wife of an adulterous monster who is having an affair with a younger woman. It's an old story. But is this really their story? If you were to ask Geoff, would he talk of years of deep-rooted unhappiness, growing apart, trying and failing to reconnect? Was Mary really still 'in' the marriage emotionally? Were they both, in fact, already in some ways living separate lives?

Furthermore, does it help or hinder Mary to be cast as the victim? Her first instinct was to start divorce proceedings. Luckily, her sister held her back. If she hadn't done so, Mary's wronged wife story could have spread like wildfire – an easy, simplistic narrative which has eviscerated all other nuances. And then what for Mary? It's not that much fun being the object of everyone's sympathy. And what about Geoff? Is he really to take all the blame? Is that fair? Of course not. Fiona was a symptom, not a cause.

So, what is the way out of this for Mary and Geoff? Well, they need to talk about their marriage. And they need time. Rushing into a legal process at this stage, when neither of them is emotionally ready, would mean their hurt, shame, anger and betrayal would be played out in the forum least equipped to deal with these conflicting feelings: the Family Court.

For most divorcing couples, the best first step is getting a counsellor or therapist in the room with them to facilitate the honest conversations which need to take place. Many couples will need individual as well as joint sessions. But the aim has to be to get to a position where both people understand why this relationship has let them down and give each other permission to move on.

So, back to your divorce and agreeing a narrative. If you can, frame it as a joint decision. When celebrities announce their divorces, there is a reason why many of them issue a joint statement: it sends a clear message that they want their divorce to be viewed as an amicable one. Obviously, human interactions almost never fit that perfect mould and, high-profile or not, when it comes to divorce you will be faced with the same emotional journey. You cannot buy your way out of it – in fact, sometimes more money makes it worse – but there are ways of making it easier.

No blame-style narrative

You don't need to agree *why* your relationship no longer works for you both, you just need to agree that it's not working.

What has led to this decision will be long and complex, and draw on years of tiny shifts in your relationship and the way you relate to each other. At the time, these can seem completely inconsequential, but they build as the years go by. Sometimes there is a trigger event, which can be quite dramatic. It is extremely easy (and oftentimes quite tempting) to attribute the divorce to that one event. But that will lead you down a path of guilt, shame and conflict. By taking out the need to agree on the results of the post-mortem, you relieve yourselves of significant pressure.

A fixed blame-style narrative which gives one cause (e.g. 'We split up because of his affair/her workload') sucks you into a trap which is hard to escape. In reality, there will be a complex web of reasons why the relationship is no longer working for you both. By allowing yourselves the freedom to look at the whole picture and each individual strand, you can retain empathy for each other, which you will need to navigate this transition well. It also means you can identify the dynamics that weren't working, so in your next relationship you can do things differently. Research suggests that three out of four divorced people go on to marry again,[6] so look on this process as an opportunity to learn, evolve and move on.

Go back to the basics. We get married because we believe we will make each other happier together than apart. Once that formula stops working, our relationship is no longer meeting our needs.

Now it is time for you to take your pursuit of happiness in another direction, while respecting the shared memories and experiences that came before. Saying that you have reached a shared decision that your marriage has come to an end says nothing about the why. You don't need to specify why. You don't owe the world an explanation.

A story of achievements

Your marriage will have had its high points. Take pride in what you have achieved. Pride may be one of the seven deadly sins. But really there are two types of pride:[7]

- The good type of pride is authentic pride, which stems from proven possession of a valued ability. It's the sense of achievement you give yourself when you know you have done a good job.

- Hubristic pride, however, is the opposite. This is the grandiose belief that you have prized qualities when, in fact, you don't. It's ego and arrogance with no actual basis.

These two very different types of pride – authentic and hubristic – produce very different outcomes. A study of 1,000 people undertaken by a team at the University of Miami led by psychologist Charles Carver found that people who habitually experience authentic pride have greater self-control, perseverance and goal attainment.[8] Those who frequently experience hubris, however, tend to be more impulsive and motivated solely by monetary or related external rewards.

Feeling authentic pride has been shown to increase effort and success at work. In an experiment led by German psychologist Wilhelm Hofmann, participants were buzzed seven times a day on their smartphones and asked if they had recently experienced any temptations they tried to avoid: procrastination, overeating, drinking alcohol, taking drugs, sleeping, etc.[9] If they had experienced a temptation, they were asked about their emotional state and whether their attempts at self-control had been effective. Hofmann found that authentic pride increased self-control: the instances in which people reported feeling more pride directly corresponded to the ones in which they resisted tempting and pleasurable behaviours that might have otherwise distracted them from their goals.

Crucially, though, for authentic pride to produce results, it must be paired with humility – an acknowledgement that no matter our skill-set, each of us depends on what others have to offer. Since none of us can be expert in all things, we must be humble enough to recognize that we cannot be great at everything. There will be times when we need to rely on others.

So how can this help us in divorce? In a number of ways:

List your achievements as a couple

There will be so many. If you can, sit down together, if not, do so on your own, get out a pen and paper and write them down. Some will be obvious: children, exciting holidays, friendships, career goals met, house moves, renovations, garden projects, pets. Some won't spring immediately to mind, but can be even more defining: in relationships, couples can give each other the strength to be brave and try new things, to face a fear, to feel loved and nurtured, to laugh, to be silly and irresponsible, to try something new, to dream. Think back to the early years and the times when things were good. Those are the memories to bank, to hold on to.

Acknowledge them

'Well done, us, for all that we have achieved!' This feeling is one of authentic pride. Allow yourself to feel it. By focusing on what you have, in the past, navigated well as a couple, you will give yourself the self-control and perseverance to achieve your goal now. That goal is to divorce well, with the minimum emotional and financial cost to you both. You have overcome challenges as a couple before. So you can do this too. Don't be distracted from that goal. You will be tempted to resort to blame and fault, but your authentic pride in what you have achieved before can help avoid those pitfalls.

Recognize that these were joint achievements

Divorce is also a shared endeavour. The only way to 'win' at divorce (that is to say, achieve a fair result with the minimum emotional and financial cost) is if you *both* win at divorce. If you can't work together to achieve a fair outcome for you both and your family, you will end up working against each other. Sadly, for some couples, this is inevitable, due to an abuse dynamic or because they just won't play fair, for instance if one tries to hide assets from the other. But, fortunately, in the vast majority of divorces, couples do not set out to destroy each other. They just want to find a solution which is fair to them both.

So, use your pride in your past achievements to value what is to come in the future. Divorce is a new challenge. You're going to nail it. And what comes next could be more exciting than anything which has gone before.

WRITING A NEW STORY, SETTING NEW GOALS

If you want to accomplish the goals of your life,
you have to begin with the spirit.

Oprah Winfrey

For many couples, freeing each other for new adventures is the hardest part. But there's no need to reject everything in the relationship. Approached right, divorce can help you preserve the parts of your relationship that still work well, but jettison the dynamics that are bringing you down. This can be particularly powerful when it comes to a co-parenting relationship, if that is your particular situation, but it may also help you work through your relationships with mutual friends and extended family members.

Inevitably, the two of you won't feel ready at the same time, and there's no point charging ahead until you are both emotionally equipped to do so.

The journey you go through on divorce is similar to that on bereavement, although unlike most bereavements your social network can fracture around you.

The divorce journey

Here are the emotional stages of divorce that many counsellors reference. The 'divorce journey' is not a linear one, so you are likely to move between these stages in a random order. The crucial point is that you both need to be at 'acceptance' to have meaningful and successful conversations about the long term, including the arrangements for your children (if you have them) and the division of your finances.

- *Denial:* You can't accept you are getting divorced. It seems surreal. Why couldn't you 'fix' the marriage? This can send you into a whirlwind of emotions which prevent you from accepting the truth. Is there something you can do to get the marriage back on track?
- *Shock:* You're not acting like yourself. You have feelings of panic. This can be compounded if you feel that you have wasted years in a marriage which has failed. What was it all for?
- *Contrasting emotions:* You can't control your emotions. You jump from hope to despair with ease. You may read a part of this book and agree with it completely today, but the words will swim in front of your eyes tomorrow. You may start obsessing about why the marriage 'failed'.
- *Bargaining:* You can still make the marriage work. You just need to change. You can do that. You may come up with extreme measures to force the other person to change their mind. It is completely natural to go through this stage. But know that you cannot control love, or someone else's happiness. *You* deserve to be happy, and that won't come from changing yourself for somebody else.
- *Letting go:* You realize that the marriage has ended and you open up to the idea that fault (whether you are blaming yourself or blaming the other person) isn't helping you. This is a good stage to start having frank and honest conversations about your divorce story and the legacy of your marriage. You may start to feel a sense of freedom and be more positive about what the future holds.
- *Acceptance:* This is the point at which the negative emotions finally stop. You accept that you are both entitled to lead a life that is filled with happiness. You will understand that there *is* life after divorce, and that there are more positive things to look forward to in your life. The way you approach divorce will dictate how quickly you reach this stage. Sadly, there are divorcing couples who never get there. If you allow the conflict of a bitterly contested and adversarial divorce to take hold, it can consume you. Don't let it.

MARY AND GEOFF

Here's the narrative that Mary and Geoff, after two months of separation counselling (together and separately), agreed on as their divorce story. It was what they told their adult children, their family members, their friends and the world. It became their mantra, and their coping mechanism at times during the divorce when they were pulling in opposite directions, particularly on the finances. But it carried them through, and stopped the story of their divorce consuming the happy story of their marriage:

> After 37 years together, we have made the joint decision that it is time for our marriage to come to an end. We are so proud of everything we have achieved together, including our amazing children and our countless shared life experiences, but it is now time for us to both move on to different adventures apart.

Your future narrative

What is coming next? What new life experiences await? Shifting to your future narrative will give your children, family and friends the lead they need to help you look forwards, not back. You are not abandoning your old relationship – it will have defined you in many ways, and if you have children you will be co-parents for life – but you are acknowledging that the relationship is no longer meeting both your needs and it's time to move on.

Don't let the world in

Once you have reached a narrative, together, which you can both accept and live with, guard it fiercely. We will speak later in the book (at Step 9) about how to manage friends and family, but a word of caution now: beware.

Approaching divorce as a shared life change to be navigated together is by far the best way for you, your children and your family. However, the stigma of divorce has a life of its own, so you will constantly need to reframe the way your friends and family view yours. No, they don't have to take sides. No, there isn't a 'villain' and a 'victim'. No, you don't want to hear how you were never compatible. You were once, thank you very much, you've just both grown apart. No, you don't necessarily want sympathy. You're doing OK. You'd quite like some humour and cocktails.

Lead the narrative and the people who care for you will follow. They're not trying to derail you, they just don't know the right things to say. Educate them. Show them Step 9 below.

Also be mindful that they will view your divorce through their own life choices. Research in social judgement has revealed that people are egocentric: they judge others in the same way that they judge themselves.[10]

Psychologists have spent decades studying the power of social influence, and the way in which it manipulates people's opinions and behaviour. Social influence is the way in which individuals change their ideas and actions to meet the demands of a social group. Most of us encounter it in its many forms on a regular basis. The majority-held opinions of a group of friends, for instance, are likely to inform the views of new members to that social group. But beware of conformity. If you conform to the social norms of a group, it means that you may disagree with the opinions that they express or the actions that they take, but nonetheless you adopt the behaviour that is expected of you.[11] So, if you have a group of friends and within that group the experience of divorce is a negative one, it may seem easier for you to fit in with that narrative. If a close friend has a terrible relationship with his former spouse, it might feel more socially acceptable to be the same, and speak negatively about yours. But in the long term that will bring you down. Be true to yourself and your own experience. If it is hard within your social group to be positive about divorce, move the conversation on. Don't let the emotional baggage of others bring you down.

In the 1950s, the Polish psychologist Solomon Asch carried out a series of experiments known as the Asch Paradigms to understand the circumstances which led to people conforming to a majority influence. In an experiment at Swarthmore College, Pennsylvania, Asch presented participants with a printed line of a given length, and a series of additional lines of varying lengths.[12] One of the lines was the same length as in the initial image, whilst the other two were significantly different. In a group setting, participants were then asked to individually report which of the lines was the same length as the first. They were unaware that other members of the group had been instructed to answer that a line which was clearly of a different length matched that of the original line.

Participants were torn between two options: should they report the answer that they had observed to be correct and contradict other members of the group? Or should they disregard their private opinion and report the answer that other group members were reporting?

Even when the correct answer was obvious, Asch found that participants would conform to the group norm and give obviously inaccurate answers.

So, what does this tell us about divorce? Well, be mindful of the personal life choices of your group of friends. If they are married, they may feel threatened by your divorce, particularly if you are doing well. It may, in a warped way, on some unconscious level, suit them if your divorce is awful. If they are divorced, they may welcome the newest crew member with a gusto which grates.

All this really reinforces is the need for the two of you to agree your narrative together. Then the perspective of the outside world becomes largely irrelevant. This is *your* story, not theirs.

Love can endure

This is a theme we will return to in Step 10, but for now it's worth letting this idea ruminate in your subconscious.

Don't allow a void to grow where love once resided, as it will be all too easy for it to be filled with resentment, guilt, anger and blame. Keep talking, respect each other and respect the love you once had for each other.

||||||||||||||||||||||||||||||||||||||||||||||||||||||||||||||||||||||||||||||||||||||||||||||||||||||||||||||||

OVER TO YOU ...

||||||||||||||||||||||||||||||||||||||||||||||||||||||||||||||||||||||||||||||||||||||||||||||||||||||||||||||||

Setting your goals

By now you should be taking on the mindset you will need to navigate your divorce well. It's time to start applying this thinking to your own family.

When the time is right for you, and you are in a calm, uninterrupted space, take out your laptop or a pen and write down the answers to these four questions. We will come back to them, and they will change as you work through the plan. Much of this book is for you to navigate together, but for this exercise, work separately and don't share your answers. These are for you alone.

What do you want to achieve from this process?
- For yourself?
- For your former partner?
- For any children you may have?
- For your network of family and friends?

Some examples to start you thinking:

'I want to leave this process knowing we are both as financially secure as we
    can be.'

'I want us to be able to look each other in the eye.'

'I want to be able to tell our friends and family not to choose sides.'

'I want to be able to tell my children, when they are grown up, that we were
    fair to each other.'

'I still want to send my former parents-in-law birthday presents, and go round
    for a cup of tea, and for that not to be strange, or awkward.'

'I want to believe that this is not a failure on my part or my former partner's
    part.'

'I want us to laugh together with our children again.'

'I want our children to know we still respect each other as their parents.'

'I want to find calm and balance again.'

'I want to look forward to what's coming.'

'I want us to agree a positive lasting legacy of our marriage.'

'I want us still to feel like a family.'

'I want to be able to call him/her at 3 a.m. when our son is running a fever
    without thinking twice.'

'I want us to be able to be at friends' parties and for it to be easy.'

'I want us both to be proud of what we have achieved.'

'I want us all to be happy.'

What do you think your reshaped family unit should look like?

Don't skip over this step if you don't have children. This is meant for everyone. You are
a family unit whether you have children or not. For many years you have been the most
important people in each other's lives. Think carefully about how you want to transition
to a relationship which is different but still reflects the important part you have each
played.

Some examples to start you thinking:

'I want to continue to share good and bad news with you, and ask for your
    advice.'

'I want us to continue that Christmas tradition we have.'

'I want us to be there for each other if something bad happens in the
    future.'
'I want us to acknowledge that we made a commitment to each other when we
    got married/had children and that some of those commitments will be life-
    long.'
'I want our friends and family to be able to invite us both to the same party.'

And if you have children:

'I want it to feel natural for our children to move between our homes.'
'I want us to communicate about the children and have each other's backs – I
    want a co-parenting ally.'
'I want to know that when the children are with each of us we are consistent
    and reinforce to them how important each parent is.'
'I want our children to know that we respect each other.'
'I want our children to see there is no drama, and this is family.'
'I want our children to look back on our divorce as an irrelevant footnote.'

What do you see as the main stumbling blocks to achieving these things?

Don't use blame here, but instead state the simple, bland facts, for example:

'We aren't talking.'
'We can't look each other in the eye.'
'I'm scared.'
'I feel guilty.'
'I'm ashamed.'
'I feel betrayed.'
'I blame him/her.'
'He/she is closed to me.'
'I don't trust him/her.'
'I don't feel we're on the same page.'
'I feel this is out of my control.'

'I'm worried about money.'

'I can't sleep.'

'I don't know what to say to the children or where to begin.'

'I'm worried about what my friends will say.'

'I don't understand the divorce process and I'm terrified of getting it
      wrong.'

'I didn't choose to be in this situation.'

What makes you feel calm?

These are going to be key techniques you use when you are feeling overwhelmed. You may well need to use them when working through this exercise.

Many of us have coping mechanisms we carry out intuitively, without even realizing that is what we're doing. But remember divorce is a huge life change. At times you will feel completely overwhelmed. You may feel in crisis. Know this is normal. Please bring in some professional support now, at the earliest stage. A counsellor or therapist will help you develop your own personal strategies for feeling calm.

Here are some ideas to get you started. The idea is that by writing down what works for you, you will own it and develop your own processes to switch off from the divorce (which you may well need to do on a regular basis):

Make a cup of tea.

Take three long breaths.

Say to yourself: 'I'm feeling overwhelmed and I need to take a break.'

Light a candle.

Go for a walk.

Try to name the emotion you are feeling, and then think about what you can do
      to manage it.

Do something you enjoy which is practical and readily accessible at home:
      cooking, gardening, colouring.

Stroke a pet, take the dog out.

Do nothing for a moment.

Listen to a podcast.

Do a guided meditation (you can find a huge selection online).

Distract yourself with something else – perhaps a big life change in another
    friend's life. Finding something that is bigger than your own divorce can
    really help.

Tell yourself a positive mantra, and repeat it several times:

'This too shall pass.'
'I've got this.'
'One step at a time.'
'I'll get there.'

Relax your body: unfurrow your brow, relax your jaw, gently roll your shoulders
    back and down and lift your chest up.

Prioritize sleep and an early night.

Say no. It isn't always the right time to talk about divorce. If you need to take a
    break, say so.

Look at something, a photo perhaps, which will make you smile.

Remember it's OK to cry. Sometimes you just need to let it out.

Listen to music you love.

Put your phone and your tech away in a drawer. Free your mind from those
    stimuli.

Limit your use of social media. Is it bringing you down? Put it on hold for a
    while. Delete the app. We all know Instagram isn't real life. Take a break
    from it.

Make a short-term plan you can look forward to: a trip to the cinema, a
    breakfast with friends.

Remember divorce may not be your choice. But the way you divorce can be.

|||||||||||||||||||||||||||||||||||||||||||||||||||||||||||||||||||||||||||||||||||||||||||||||||||||||||||||||||

That's it. You've done the first exercise and finished Step 1. Well done.
Now save your answers on your computer or put them safely away
where prying eyes cannot find them. We will return to them again
later. If you'd like to share some of these thoughts with your former
partner, you can, but we're not expecting you to do so. Blow your

nose, wipe your eyes, light a scented candle or listen to some Metallica (whatever works for you!) and switch off from these heavy subjects. Your unconscious brain will do the work now, without you even realizing.

As and when you feel ready, you can look at Step 2.

STEP 2

|||||||||||||||||||||||||||||||||||||||||||||||||||||||||||||||||||||||||||||

AGREEING OUR PLAN OF ACTION

|||||||||||||||||||||||||||||||||||||||||||||||||||||||||||||||||||||||||||||

'Can't we just fall out?'
Why working together matters

Before we go any further, we need you to understand a little bit more about *why* you're working so hard to divorce well. And to understand that, you need to know the basics of what happens if you end up in Court. Don't worry, this book is not, you will be relieved to hear, remotely heavy on the law. But to make informed choices about your divorce, you absolutely do need to know what's out there.

In this step we're going to look at how the Family Court works, what it can and can't do, and what to expect if you end up there. Then we're going to begin to think about what you should be doing instead …

THE FAMILY COURT

We family lawyers are going through something of an existential crisis at the moment. What are we actually *doing* and what is the Family Court *for*? Are we making things better or worse? As we'll see, a lot of research has been done recently into whether our Family Justice system is fit for purpose (spoiler: it isn't, and it knows it isn't).

The central problem is that the process for resolving family arrangements is *adversarial*, i.e. it pits former partners against each other.

What do we mean by this?

- If negotiations fail, legal proceedings are started by one of you making an 'application' to the Court for a decision in your favour. Your application might be about arrangements for your children,[1] or your finances[2] (known as a 'financial remedy' application), or if you are particularly unlucky, both.
- Your former partner will 'respond' to the application. If you can afford lawyers, you may each be represented. Otherwise you are on your own.
- There will probably be at least two short hearings to see if the issues can be narrowed between you and to work out what evidence is needed before the Court is in a position to reach a decision. Eventually, if you don't manage to settle along the way, you may both find yourself giving evidence to the Court. This may include being cross-examined by each other's lawyers, or, if you don't have lawyers, sometimes by each other.
- Having considered the evidence and the arguments, a Judge will come to a decision and impose an outcome which, unless you roll the dice on an appeal (although in most cases you will need to be given permission to appeal before you can try), you will have to live with whether you like it or not.

It is hard to convey what this feels like for families. Let's consider how it might play out in practice.

PETER AND GABRIELA

Peter, a British citizen, and Gabriela, a Spanish citizen, live in Leeds and have been married for eight years, but want to separate. They have two children, aged 6 and 4. Gabriela has not worked since their first child was born, but has mentioned that she is thinking of trying to get back into work as a freelance web designer. Peter works for an advertising agency. Tensions are running high, as Peter is worried that Gabriela wants to relocate with the children back to Madrid, where her parents live. Gabriela insists she hasn't made her mind up yet, but hasn't ruled it out.

The immediate issue is money. Gabriela wants to move out of the family home as soon as possible and rent somewhere nearby. Peter says he cannot afford to pay rent and that if she wants to move out, she should get a job. He says his mother can help with childcare if need be. Unfortunately Gabriela doesn't trust Peter's mother after a row they had about the separation.

To see if there's a way forward, Gabriela decides to instruct a solicitor, who writes to Peter. Despite the calm and polite tone of the letter, Peter feels defensive and under pressure. Gabriela has made it clear she doesn't want to talk about the issues directly with him because it always ends in an argument, but Peter feels he can't afford his own solicitor.

Gabriela's solicitors set out her proposals and suggest mediation. Peter is asked to respond. But he doesn't know how the Court decides these issues and is unsure what to say, anxious that whatever he does say will be the wrong thing and used against him. In the absence of any progress, Gabriela's solicitors issue an application to the Family Court. Unfortunately, because the Court is so busy, a hearing cannot take place for three months.

The family is stuck. Gabriela can't move out because she doesn't have the money, and is increasingly desperate. She tells Peter that she has decided that she does now want to move back to Spain. Peter is distraught and begins to dread opening his emails in case there is another communication from Gabriela's solicitors.

With the hearing approaching, Peter decides to bite the bullet and hires his own lawyers. With the help of both sets of lawyers, Gabriela and Peter agree a rental solution for the next 12 months for Gabriela. But this is only the beginning. They still have to tackle the much bigger long-term decisions of whether their children should relocate to Spain with Gabriela and how to divide up the family finances.

The 12-month rental agreement has been an expensive exercise, emotionally as well as financially (we'll come on to the question of cost shortly). It has also significantly eroded trust. Each feels the other has behaved unreasonably. Neither has really attempted to consider the other's point of view. Neither feels that the ground is well prepared for the much bigger decisions that await them about the arrangements for their children and their finances.

Had the Court hearing gone ahead, Gabriela and Peter would have found their case listed as *Gabriela v Peter*. This is not just some terminological relic from days gone by – it's scrupulously accurate. If you go to Court, you are regarded as being 'against' each other. Barristers are 'opponents' and your solicitors will usually refer to your former partner's team as 'the other side'.

It is worth bearing in mind that solicitors' professional conduct rules require them to act in the best interests of their respective clients, not of the family as a whole. But the Judge's job is quite different: in a financial case like this, they have to strive to be fair to *both* parties.

Exactly the same point can be made about cases concerning disputed arrangements for children. Your lawyers will prepare and deploy the arguments they hope will be successful to achieve the ends you seek. But the Judge has to identify what is in the children's best interests. As Sir James Munby, former president of the Family Division (the most senior Family Judge in England and Wales), pointed out back in 2015:

> the Court proceeds, if one bothers to think about what is going on, and most of the time we do not, on the blithe assumption that the truth – and a proper appraisal of what is in the child's best interests – will in some mysterious way emerge from the adversarial process between the parents.[3]

This isn't the place for a root and branch re-examination of the principles of our ancient legal system, but the point is a fair one, isn't it? Why *do* we assume that pitting arguments against each other will necessarily result in good outcomes? In some cases, it may simply reveal the best lawyers. For families at least, adversariality is a peculiar starting-point.

Put another way, there is a crucial disjunction between the tasks confronting the lawyers (presenting the best arguments in the most attractive light) and the Court (making an objective assessment of what the answer should be). And one does not necessarily help the other.

So, what do the Family Justice professionals think?

In November 2020, the Family Solutions Group, a group of professionals working in the field, including Judges, lawyers, mediators, family therapists and academics, took the latest in a series of long hard looks at the Family Justice system. Their report puts the point like this:

> In a private family law dispute where legal representation can be afforded privately, the interests of the two parents are legally represented, but the child(ren)'s interests are not, generally, legally represented. It may well be reassuring for parents to have a professional 'on their side', but this leads to a parent-centric system rather than one centred on the overall family needs.[4]

And later on:

> Given the well-established advantages for children of parents who communicate and manage successful cooperative parenting, it is important to distinguish between a process in which parents are working together to find a resolution and those in which the parents are set against each other. Solicitors may have a good working relationship and manage a civilized process between them for resolving their clients' issues, but the process itself might be one where the parents are represented against each other.[5]

So there you have it: the structure of the Court system provides support to parents individually at the expense of the family as a whole. And, while the above quotes focus on families with children, the same is true for those without – an environment which pitches individuals against each other is rarely going to result in a positive outcome.

No one involved in Family Justice really doubts how inappropriate this set-up is any more. 'Winning' and 'losing' might be fair enough in the context of a contract or employment dispute (just), but these are profoundly unhelpful labels to apply to a separated family. It may feel great at the time, but the point about families is that, whether you like it or not, they remain families after divorce. They have to see and talk to each other for years and sometimes decades afterwards.

Or, as the most senior Family Judge in England and Wales, Sir Andrew McFarlane, put it in 2019:

> Cases of straightforward relationship dysfunction, not involving abuse or a need for protection, should not need to come before a Magistrate or Judge for resolution. Indeed, because, for this group of cases, the issues concern matters of emotion and psychology, a Court is most unlikely to be the best place to achieve any lasting resolution. The Court, with its clunky legalistic approach, will undoubtedly, in the end, produce a result which may then have to be imposed upon the parents, but, I would suggest, for this substantial group of cases, the Court process is not one that either adds value to the welfare of the child or is in any way beneficial for the parents. In some cases, it may simply provide a pitch and a referee for them to play out further rounds in their adult contest.[6]

Granted, this might matter less if you don't have children. You might *want* a pitch and a referee. But few amongst us, unless revenge is our thing, actually want to increase the temperature rather than reduce it. How does that help us move on? And even if revenge *is* your thing, you probably won't achieve the catharsis you seek. As Martin Luther King Jr said, 'An eye for an eye leaves everyone blind.'

Let's be crystal clear: in our experience the overwhelming majority of family lawyers are dedicated to minimizing the impact of family breakdown, but what we have here is essentially a problem of *structure*. The system is built wrong for families.

And before the cynics pipe up to say that the lawyers aren't going hungry on the back of all this misery, consider a recent survey by Resolution,[7] which found that in May 2021, thanks to well-being concerns, more than *a quarter of Family Justice professionals were actively considering leaving the profession altogether*. Nor can this all be laid at the door of Covid-19: more than half had considered leaving in the last three years. 'Vicarious trauma' is increasingly recognized in family law practitioners,[8] reflecting the harmful impact of managing all this conflict. And if that is the effect on the trained professionals, who are involved in these cases at one remove, then we do have to ask ourselves: what is the likely effect on the families themselves?

'But what if I just want to go to Court anyway?'

Then be aware before you get there that the feeling is not mutual … The Family Court really doesn't want to see you unless you are in genuine need. Of course, its *raison d'être* is to provide a forum for decisions to be taken if you really are unable to take them yourselves. But, as with many of our public services, it was hardly in rude health before Covid-19, and it has deteriorated fast since. Again, the Family Solutions Group report:

> The 'Family Justice System' is in crisis. This is no exaggeration. The numbers of parents making applications are unmanageable and Family Courts are stretched beyond limits, with the numbers of applications (often about matters that should never have reached the doors of the Court) growing exponentially. The system is recognized as broken and in need of radical reform. The Family Justice Reform Implementation Group has been tasked with formulating proposals for an overhaul of the system. However, this will take time.[9]

And if you go to Court when the Judge considers you should not have
… well, heed this warning from His Honour Judge Wildblood in 2020:

> Do not bring your private law litigation to the Family Court here unless it is
> genuinely necessary for you to do so. You should settle your differences (or
> those of your clients) away from Court, except where that is not possible. If you
> do bring unnecessary cases to this Court, you will be criticised, and sanctions
> may be imposed upon you. There are many other ways to settle disagreements,
> such as mediation.[10]

The Judge in that case had expressed his continuing dismay over
having to decide such trivialities as which junction of the M4 motor-
way should serve as the handover location for the children, and the
exact time for children to be returned on a Sunday. Faced with an
unrelenting diet of really serious cases, involving child protection
issues in particular, it is understandable that judicial patience is wear-
ing thin. Why should scarce public resources be expended in this
manner, when the system is in crisis? Which would explain recent
reports that the Lord Chancellor is considering the introduction of
financial penalties for parents who clog up the Court system unnecessarily.[11]

Be aware that the rules of procedure that govern family cases
already require the Court to consider at every stage of proceedings
whether a case is suitable for resolution elsewhere – by the parties
working constructively together, if possible. We all expect this to be
enforced more rigorously in future, meaning that even if you go to
Court, you can't guarantee that a Judge won't adjourn the case to
encourage you to engage in out-of-Court processes first to attempt to
settle.

WORKING TOGETHER

So, having peeked over the fence at what the Court experience has to offer (and rapidly retreated), back to you. The good news is help is at hand.

There are now a range of increasingly sophisticated out-of-Court options for families, which enable a more civilized, quicker, cheaper approach. All of them depend on one factor, however: working together. It doesn't sound easy, and it isn't. But, unless you are one of the very few couples who genuinely require a Judge and a Courtroom, this is what you should be doing.

What do we mean by 'working together'?

At its core, this means setting goals which you both want to achieve. You cannot expect another person to work with you towards a goal they do not want or care about. How do you go about it?

- Start expansively. Think big picture. What are you likely to be able to agree on? How about not spending a fortune on lawyers?! That's a good start. Reaching a settlement you can both live with. Not spending the next two years of your lives embroiled in litigation. Being able to tell your children you have been fair to each other. If you ignore the specifics for now, you're likely to find that your broad goals are aligned.
- Take ownership of the divorce process and of the decisions you will need to make, rather than delegating this vital function to lawyers and Judges.
- Try to see things from each other's perspective. Be constructive.
- Don't dogmatically insist on your red lines. In fact, please don't set any red lines. The right answer for the family as a whole will emerge. Don't put barriers up to that process.
- Don't rush off to see lawyers in a panic unless you really have to. Working together is about taking sensible professional advice and applying it to your

family in a measured way. Settling your case at the door of the Court isn't working together, it's crisis management.

- Start as you mean to continue. This is your divorce and your life. It will be an intensely personal and sometimes painful process. But with the right mindset and the right support you can do it. And you can do it together. There really isn't a sensible alternative.

Depending on when you realized things were 'over', you may already have reached some tentative conclusions about how you want the future to look. Equally, you might not have the faintest idea. That's absolutely fine – there's plenty of time, and if you take away anything from this book, it should be that divorce is a process not to be rushed or delayed, but taken at your own pace.

But either way, you will be forgiven if there is still a voice in your head whispering, or maybe even shouting, 'But we're getting divorced! The whole point is we're supposed to be separating … to be free to do what we want. Do we really have to work together?' That would be perfectly understandable.

When it comes to your divorce, there are lots of good reasons why you may not be attracted to the idea of cooperating.

For a start, friends and family often don't get it. If you're so good at working together, then why are you splitting up? Well-meaning friends who have been through the Court process may lack the knowledge and objectivity to understand why you aren't just aiming for 'the best deal you can get' from a Judge, as they did. They may not want to admit to themselves how destructive that process was for their own family, with all the associated feelings of guilt that might involve. There may be a genuine concern that you are selling yourself short.

And the old-fashioned way of dealing with a divorce by just 'leaving it to the lawyers' is so much easier emotionally, right? Couples can simply delegate responsibility to their advisers to sort it out for them, whilst responding to the odd telephone call and email as they go about their new lives. And if things get a bit heated with the ex, that's just par for the course …

We've already considered with Gabriela and Peter how things can be blown off-course quite quickly if you aren't careful. To work together, you have to keep communicating. If you're talking to each other, then you can reassure each other about your motivations, and what you are each seeking. If you're not, mistrust can soon build. And if you don't work together, you'll most likely end up working against each other. Fundamentally, divorce requires a shared solution.

Naturally, where you stand on the need-to-work-together spectrum will depend on your individual circumstances. If you met online and after a whirlwind romance eloped to Las Vegas and now, following a ceremony you barely remember, have been married for 5 minutes and have no children, no friends in common and no indelibly tattooed declarations of love, it's understandable if you feel less invested in busting a gut to keep things amicable post-divorce. On the other hand, if you have children together, everything changes.

But whoever you are and whatever your circumstances, divorcing positively will help you leave the relationship feeling good about the way you have handled it, which in turn will help you to move on.

'What if we don't communicate well at the best of times …?'

If you are both already at the stage of accepting your marriage has ended, communication will be much easier for that reason alone. You'll both be looking forward, with a common purpose. But many couples who have reached that point and do like the idea of working together in principle still lack confidence in their ability to do so in practice.

A perceived inability to *communicate* will often have been at the very heart of the decision to separate, at least for one of you. Communication issues are frequently cited as a key driver for divorce, from which so much else then flows: lack of intimacy, lack of respect or sympathy, lack of trust, or simply growing apart. In a 2019 Danish study,[12] 44 per cent of respondents reported communication problems as a major contributing factor in their separation. Our experience would suggest this is an underestimate, if anything. You can construct a reasonable argument to say that practically every routine cause of divorce starts with a failure of communication of one kind or another.

Fortunately, though, simply deciding you both want to communicate about your divorce will begin the process. We'll address what further support you may need as we move through this book.

Of course, as with all compromises, working together is difficult – the old cliché in family law circles is that if both sides are a bit unhappy with the outcome, then the Judge has probably got it right – but it is overwhelmingly the best way:

- To retain a measure of control over the process, rather than being carried along by events.
- To ensure privacy.
- To promote better outcomes for yourself and your children, if you have them.
- To save money.
- To save time, so you can get on with moving on.

Let's look at these in a bit more detail:

You retain control

The Court process is deeply disempowering. You have very little control over the cost, you are at the mercy of the Court's diary when it comes to timing, and of course, at the end of the day a Court Order is imposed upon you, which you may or may not like (but let's be realistic: you probably won't love it). You are essentially a passenger in a process you will hate but for which you will pay lavishly.

Working together offers a way out of all of that:

- You have discussions at a time which suits you and your family. That means you don't have to take time off work (or have discussions with your employer) for Court hearings, or arrange childcare.
- You can opt for face-to-face or remote discussions.
- You can build in time for reflection, and for accessing other helpful support along the way (*see* Step 3) – counselling or co-parenting sessions, perhaps.
- You can pause your discussions in order to deal with other pressing aspects of life – maybe the children have exams or are starting a new school. Maybe you have a new job, or just need a break.

In short, you can work at a pace which suits you.

You can ensure privacy

Be aware that the Family Court can and does permit journalistic scrutiny of its decisions and, in certain circumstances, reporting – and increasingly so. As a High Court Judge, Mr Justice Holman, observed back in 2014, 'There is a huge legitimate public interest in open justice in family cases, just as much as in criminal, or in civil cases,'[13] before quoting Jeremy Bentham:

> Publicity is the very soul of justice. It is the keenest spur to exertion and the surest of all guards against improbity. It keeps the Judge himself, while trying, under trial.[14]

This is not the place for a detailed examination of the rules in this area, but in general terms, accredited members of the media are allowed to attend Court hearings unless the Judge says otherwise. The extent to which they are then permitted to publish details of the proceedings has been subject to a wide-ranging review, the Family Division's Transparency Review,[15] which concluded in October 2021 and is currently being implemented.

Better outcomes for you and your family

You probably don't need a truckload of academic research to persuade you that an acrimonious divorce is going to have an impact on your general well-being, not to mention your finances. But at the risk of stating the obvious, it will. And the effects on any children can be long term.

Consider an interesting recent study,[16] which asked employees at 133 workplaces across the UK about their experiences of relationship breakdown. One of its findings was that 60 per cent of respondents suffered an impact on their mental health and another that just under 10 per cent left their employment within a year of divorce. These findings chime with a 2014 study for the *Nashville Business Journal*,[17] which found that in the 6 months leading up to and in the year of divorce, an employee's productivity was reduced by 40 per cent and would suffer on some level *for the next 5 years*.

It's a constant bugbear of ours that employers can and should be doing much more to support their employees, not just because it's the right thing to do, but also *because it's transparently in their own interest to do so*. But that aside, the wider point is that it just isn't possible to compartmentalize divorce as a simply personal issue – if poorly handled, it has the potential to cross-contaminate every area of your existence, even those you might regard as purely 'professional'. The impact of divorce doesn't stop when you clock in at work.

What about the impact on children?

An influential report from the highly respected Nuffield Foundation in January 2019[18] came to the conclusion that 38 per cent of separating families end up in Court disputing arrangements for their children, destroying the cosy prior assumption that the proportion was a more manageable (though still ridiculous) 1 in 10. Whilst there is some debate about the assumptions underpinning the data that led to that figure, that is a staggering statistic if even only approximately accurate.

Leaving aside the considerable problem of resourcing all these cases with a functioning Courtroom and Judge, the principal concern is the impact on the children of all this litigation.

A huge amount of research has been done in recent years by academics and family law professionals about the impact of parental conflict on families. *How* you separate is crucial. The evidence is that it is not just the relationships between each parent and their child that matter (though they are obviously vital), but also the relationship between the adults.

Put simply, children benefit from their parents having a functioning relationship and are disadvantaged if they do not, in a way that can impact their mental health long term.[19]

Consider this helpful summary on the gov.uk website:[20]

Frequent, intense and poorly resolved conflict between parents can place children at risk of mental health issues, and behavioural, social and academic problems. It can also have a significant effect on a child's long-term outcomes.

There is a strong body of evidence to show how damaging inter-parental conflict can:

- harm children's outcomes, even when parents manage to sustain positive parent–child relationships
- put children at more risk of:
  - » having problems with school and learning
  - » negative peer relationships
  - » physical health problems
  - » smoking and substance misuse
  - » mental health and well-being challenges
- The risks can also have an effect on long-term life outcomes such as:
  - » poor future relationship chances
  - » reduced academic attainment
  - » lower employability

> » heightened interpersonal violence
> » depression and anxiety

The importance of getting this right cannot really be overstated.

You'll save money

So … what does it cost to get divorced? Cost is important. Please note that we're not talking (yet) about financial settlements, i.e. how your assets are divided, maintenance payments, etc. (we'll consider these in detail in Step 8), but about the costs of the *process* of divorcing.

There is an enduring level of confusion about what divorce actually is in this context. Divorce proceedings themselves are simply the process by which you change your official status from 'married' to 'divorced' (and similarly for civil partners). Aside from the fee you pay to the government for the privilege of processing the paperwork, weighing in at a chunky £593 as we write, the divorce proceedings themselves are not usually where the money gets spent. This is because spouses usually agree that they want to get divorced, so there is no expensive dispute which needs resolving. We'll look at this too in more detail in Step 4.

Instead, when people talk about the costs of divorce, they are generally referring to the costs of arguing about their money (known as 'financial remedy proceedings') or their children, or both.

Over the years, there have been a number of attempts to put a figure on the 'average' legal costs of 'divorce' to families. Back in 2017, a family law firm[21] put the average cost at £9,000 per couple, or £19,000 for couples in London, figures which can only have risen since. The Money Advice Service[22] puts the figure at £30,000 + VAT 'or more' for a financial remedy application that goes all the way to trial. But with due respect to these figures, speculating in this area is difficult. Differing family circumstances throw up different issues upon divorce: your case may be very unlike another.

As barristers dealing with cases through to the end, we are in a good position to see what the costs of litigation are, and how they have arisen. It is not at all uncommon to find the costs of contested litigation in relatively 'ordinary' financial remedy cases approaching £50,000 on each side by the time of a final hearing, and in more complex cases well into six figures on each side.

For better-off families, that represents a hell of a lot of discretionary spending which now won't be happening. For the less well-off, there will be a colossal and lasting impact on their future standard of living – there will be a lot less to spend on, say, rehousing within a postcode which is convenient for the school run, or going on a much-needed holiday, or replacing the car.

Equally, if there is no other means of paying, one or both parties may have to leave the marriage with significant debts on their shoulders.

The Court process is expensive if for no other reason than there is a *lot* of to-ing and fro-ing between the lawyers. A letter is sent and received. Your instructions are taken before a response is drafted for you to consider. You give further instructions on the draft letter. Your letter is eventually sent and received by the other side. And then the same thing happens all over again. That's an awful lot of lawyer time being committed to the business of basic communication.

And the costs of Court proceedings are essentially unpredictable. Solicitors are obliged to (and do) try their best to give a good idea of what the costs will be at various stages of the litigation, but the accuracy of their estimate is liable to be undermined by factors beyond their control. To return to Gabriela and Peter for a moment, what happens if Gabriela decides she needs a break and wants to take the children to Spain for a holiday, but Peter disagrees on the basis that the Covid-19 regulations in place at the time are unlikely to permit it? This could easily lead to protracted correspondence, and possibly even a further application to the Court – all at additional, and unbudgeted for, expense.

A WARNING: *M V M* [2020]

As a salutary reminder of how things can spiral out of control, consider this case. After nearly 22 years of marriage, which, as the Judge observed, 'must have contained happy times together,' and having had three children, the divorcing couple embarked on 'ruinous and recriminatory' financial remedy proceedings. After 13 hearings, the combined legal costs were £594,000 and the litigation had led to fractured relations between the children and their father.

By the time of the trial, the only asset was the proceeds of the sale of the family home, £630,000, which, after the repayment of debts (including legal fees), left the couple just £5,000 each.

As the Judge put it, 'There may be worse examples of disproportionate and ill-judged litigation, but none spring readily to mind.'

By contrast, working together promotes compromise. It puts you in the best possible position to identify issues early on and decide what help you need to resolve them and to understand how to approach potentially contentious points with an understanding of and respect for each other's point of view. And increasingly, legal advice can be given for a fixed fee, particularly if you share a lawyer, rather than on an open-ended hourly rate.

The key point on cost is that by working together you retain an element of control. You are not dependent on the litigation strategy of the other side to keep things affordable.

You'll save time

Separating well is something which can't be rushed, but nor should it languish. After all, you are trying to create the conditions for moving forward. For some, that will happen quickly. Others will need more time. But what nobody needs is time taken up unnecessarily by the practicalities of separating.

Usually, it is not the divorce itself that is especially time-consuming, but the resolution of matters to do with money or children. Particularly money.

According to the insurers Aviva,[23] the average length of time taken to resolve financial matters upon divorce is 14.5 months (3 months longer than in 2014). It's worth taking a moment to reflect on what that feels like in real life. Whilst the finances remain unresolved, most families will not have the most basic building blocks of their future life in place. For example, unless you know your housing budget, how can you deal with the geography? Where will you be able to afford to live? How will that affect your work? Will the children's current schooling arrangements be impacted? Will you be able to live close enough to your former partner to make co-parenting the reality you want?

Unless you can find another way, and assuming Aviva is correct, you will be carrying these imponderables around for over a year. Obviously, that is likely to be incredibly stressful and unsettling. It is also likely to subject your relationship with your former partner to a significant degree of pressure.

And as ever, the Court is the very slowest of all the routes to certainty. Working together is the quickest.

Hopefully we've persuaded you that working together isn't merely an option but a necessity. Over the course of the book we're going to be pinpointing practical ways and strategies for you to weave that overriding aim into the fabric of the way you divorce and the processes you choose.

There's no exercise for you to do at the end of this step, because what we're focusing on here is mindset. But what we would say is this: know that working together is harder than working against each other. All your instincts will push you the other way. So when you are being pulled in opposite directions, pop back to this step and reread a little of it. Hopefully, it will help you both get back on track.

And when you're ready, let's move on to Step 3, which is all about the professional support you might need to help you reach an agreement you both consider fair.

STEP 3

||||||||||||||||||||||||||||||||||||||||||||||||||||||||||||||||||||||

DECIDING WHAT PROFESSIONAL SUPPORT WE NEED

||||||||||||||||||||||||||||||||||||||||||||||||||||||||||||||||||||||

'Will we need more than just a lawyer?
Do we need a lawyer at all?'

Here, we are going to set out all the different professionals who are available to you, the benefits and pitfalls of each, and how they all work together.

Hopefully you're now both at the stage where you see the benefits of working together through the divorce process and you've started to build a picture of your current financial situation and goals for the future.

So, what next?

Don't try to jump straight to the answer

Pause. Stop that train of thought. It is almost inevitable at this point that the specifics of your goals will start to diverge. Yes, you can agree that you want to be decent, fair, transparent and set a good example to the children. But you also want to stay living in the family home/repay that money you borrowed 10 years ago from your parents/not go back to work until the children are at secondary school/reassure your business partner that the divorce will have no impact on your shareholding/ figure out how you are going to manage the forthcoming bookings for the children's summer holidays.

This is where we come back to red lines, and how utterly counter-productive they are. You will both have different priorities. Of course you will! It's extremely stressful being in a state of transition and being unable to plan for the future. Whenever we meet divorcing couples (and we always meet them individually first to make sure they are suitable for a joint service), they are crying out for *answers*.

So the sooner we can get you to a place where you have some certainty as to what the future will hold, at least in the short term, the better.

And that is where professional advice comes in.

WHY PROFESSIONAL SUPPORT HELPS

The reason you are both instinctively reaching different answers isn't because one of you is reasonable and the other is not – far from it. It's because the answers can be hard to find. And you each may be follow-ing different, but equally flawed, logic.

You probably haven't been through a divorce before. And if you have, it will have been entirely different from this one. Because every divorce is unique. In the way that every relationship is unique. What you've learned about your neighbour's divorce won't help you a jot when it comes to your own. In fact, it may lead you down an entirely unhelpful rabbit hole.

Isn't there just one answer?

No. Crucially, you should know that there isn't *one right answer*. We have over 35 years' family law experience between us and even *we* don't immediately know the answer to every case.

MARK AND DAVID

Mark and David are both in their late thirties. They got married two years ago. They had been in a relationship for five years before they got married, although they hadn't lived together.

At the time of the marriage Mark ran his own business and David was employed as a social worker. They got married because they wanted to start a family. Things moved quickly: they bought a house together and started the surrogacy process. But sadly, their surrogacy arrangement broke down, putting considerable stress on their relationship. Living together didn't help. It turned out that they got on much better living apart.

So, they reached a joint decision that the marriage wasn't working and they should get divorced. They started out well, telling their friends and family together and being completely aligned in wanting to ensure that the divorce was a transition which didn't destroy everything that had gone before. But their good intentions have now started to test them. Because they have very different ideas about what is fair with regards to the finances.

Mark's view is that the situation is very straightforward: this was a short marriage and they should each take out what they put in. Sadly, they didn't have children together, so they don't have any dependants. Mark's business is doing very well and he paid the full deposit and all the mortgage payments for their home, whilst David made no financial contributions to it. So Mark thinks it's only fair that he keeps that property. Before they married, David had always rented, and so he could go back to renting again.

Mark feels that David's resistance to this proposal shows he is motivated by money. Mark's friends have warned him against letting David 'take him to the cleaners'. This was a short marriage with no children after all.

David's perception is that they made a commitment to each other when they got married with the intention that this would be long term. He took a sabbatical from his job as a social worker to focus full time on their plans to start a family. He wasn't in a position to make any financial contribution to their joint expenses, but he feels Mark's tunnel vision focus on the money fails to recognize all the other sacrifices and contributions he made to their relationship. He is in a worse financial position now than he was before they were married as, by taking a sabbatical, he missed out on the opportunity of promotion. He is aware that Mark's business had a particularly profitable period during the marriage, as Mark told him about it at the time. Their home is in joint names. David feels it would be fair for them to split it equally, so that he could share in the increase in value of Mark's business during the marriage, and for Mark to pay him maintenance, as he will never be able to earn enough to live to the same standard as Mark.

Both David and Mark have justifiable positions. But they are miles apart. It is easy to see how this could quickly escalate if they don't get a joint understanding of the legal landscape and what a Family Judge is likely to consider fair in their situation.

||||||||||||||||||||||||||||||||||||||||||||||||||||||||||||||||||||||||||||||||||||||||||||||||||||||||||||||||||||||||||||||||||||||||||

We'll look in much more detail in Step 8 at what the law says, but there are a few points it's good to get out there as early as possible:

- For any agreement you reach on your finances to be binding into the future, you will need to ask a Family Judge to convert it into a Court Order. That isn't a rubber stamp process. The Family Judge will need to be satisfied that your agreement is fair to you both, and any children you have. So the sooner you know what a Family Judge would view as fair, the better.
- Family law is a 'discretionary' jurisdiction. What this means is that there are no set formulae for working out the answer, for instance the amount of maintenance one spouse pays to the other, or how you divide up your pensions. The benefit of this is that a Family Judge is not constrained and can

find the right, bespoke outcome for you as a family. The downside is that we, as family lawyers, have to navigate a huge amount of case law (seeing what other Judges have done in scenarios that are similar to your own) to give you some certainty about what is likely to be viewed as fair for your own family.

- When it comes to any children you have, the law is firmly of the view that the best people to make decisions about your children are you. So, unlike with respect to your finances, you will never need a Court Order confirming the arrangements for your children, provided you both agree what they should be. But agreeing can be hard.

The point of this list is really this: when it comes to divorce, expertise is a good thing. You are very likely to need some professional help to navigate this well and get to the right outcomes for your family as a whole. Fortunately, you have a lot of options – many more than most people realize. The key is ensuring that you choose the right professionals for you, and that they work with you to reach a fair agreement. If the professionals helping you are making the situation worse and creating more division between you, think seriously about whether this is helping you achieve your aims or hindering you. As you will see, you are inundated with choice. Don't be afraid to move around. You can also dip in and out of expertise as and when you need it.

'SO, WHO CAN HELP US?'

Our aim is that at the end of this step you'll be able to discuss what professional support you might need and when. You can then build a timeline and a budget for those professionals, so you start to control how long your divorce is going to take and how much it is going to cost.

Importantly, we have set these professionals out in the order in which we think you should consider them. Note that lawyers aren't necessarily the first people we want you to call!

Emotional support

Marriage or separation counsellors

Why?

It can take time to work out whether this faultline in your relationship can be remedied or not. Equally, you may both be clear that the marriage has come to an end, but want to learn how to talk to each other about it. For some couples, getting a neutral, therapeutically trained third party in the room enables them to discuss deep-rooted emotions in a calm and measured way.

Cost?

Normally charged per session on an hourly rate.

Joint?

Yes.

Time-frame?

It's worth having a discussion with the counsellor at the outset to agree an initial number of sessions. If you aren't seeing the benefits after three sessions, it may be worth moving on.

Benefits?

Whether you stay married or decide the marriage has run its course, communication between the two of you is going to be key. So any process which gets you talking is great. Sometimes an open conversation can help you both move on from the difficulties you have been struggling to overcome, or can make you both at peace with the fact that your marriage has now run its course. A professional can help structure these conversations to avoid getting side-tracked and help you both manage your emotions, which will be running high.

Pitfalls?

Be wary of accessing services that propose to 'save' your marriage if that isn't what you actually want. If your marriage is making you both desperately unhappy, it's not time to resuscitate it.

Make sure you are honest with each other before you start the counselling: if one of you is quite clear in your own mind that the relationship is at an end, then have a frank discussion about that before you start. You may well be better off choosing a counsellor who offers separation counselling as well as marriage counselling (most will), to help you both navigate the emotions around the ending of your marriage.

Individual therapists

Why?

Some parts of divorce need to be navigated together, but at the same time this is a transition for you as an individual. Whether the divorce is your choice or not, you may well need some emotional support to help you make sense of your conflicting emotions. Friends and family may provide that role, but be careful not to over-share. It may feel hard to imagine, but you *will* move on in time. And once you do, you may wish you hadn't shared quite so much with your inner circle. No matter how supportive your friends and family are, there are risks in relying solely on those who know you both. We have already talked about the issues with social conformity and bias in Step 1. A professional will provide you with an opportunity to step outside your normal circle.

Cost?

Normally charged per session on an hourly rate.

Joint?

No.

Time-frame?

For some, therapy lasts for many years. But it really can be a short intervention when you need it. Be clear about your objectives and your total budget before you begin.

Benefits?

When you are under intense emotional stress, your brain checks into 'fight or flight' mode. In that state, you simply cannot engage with the long-term nuanced decisions and compromises that are needed to divorce well. Getting the right support to put you into the right frame of mind can make a huge difference.

Pitfalls?

Try not to allow therapy to become a crutch. Unless it's completely unavoidable, you want this to be short-term support, rather than long-term dependence. Having said that, if you need long-term support, you are much better off getting it from a therapist than a lawyer!

Divorce coaches

Why?

Divorce coaching is a relatively new service which can play an excellent supportive role. Generally the coaches have some history of divorce, either through experiencing it themselves or having worked as a divorce lawyer in the past. They will be able to give wraparound care and support at a much lower hourly rate than a lawyer, and can be a great sounding board.

Cost?

Varies. Many divorce coaches still work on hourly rates, but in our experience most are open to fixed fees for set pieces of work, for instance supporting you with your financial disclosure (*see* Step 6), or being paid a retainer for a set period of time. Again, have a frank discussion at the outset about your budget and what you want to achieve. Most divorce coaches will welcome clarity as to their role, and you need to take a decision in the round about how much you spend on each professional involved in your divorce.

Joint?

Divorce coaches used to work only with one spouse or the other, but there is now a growing number who work with couples. If you can manage it, transparency between you as a couple is key here. If one of you is struggling emotionally more than the other, it's worth having a conversation about how you can both best manage that. You may well agree that one of you should engage with a divorce coach on your own, or that you should start as a couple for the first couple of sessions before one continues alone. As always, what you want to avoid if at all possible is the idea that you are going off into separate teams to 'out-strategize' each other. If one of you needs more support than the other, that's fine, and it's going to help you both in the long run to reach a fair, mutually agreeable settlement if you are both emotionally ready to make those big decisions and concessions.

Time-frame?

There are three main periods in which divorce coaches can become involved: the early stages of divorce, when you are navigating the emotional fallout; mid-divorce, when you are getting through the legal, co-parenting and financial processes; and post-divorce, if you would like help and encouragement to find the 'new you'. Again, think carefully about your objectives and budget before you start.

Benefits?

Increasingly, divorce coaches are supporting family solicitors, largely because it is so much more cost-efficient to use the services of a divorce coach than a lawyer for the more straightforward aspects of divorce, or for emotional support, as they have much lower hourly rates. So a divorce coach can be a great option as your first port of call when you are having a wobble, or for helping you with getting your financial documentation together.

Pitfalls?

Please remember that a divorce coach isn't able to give you legal advice. So be very careful to identify those issues where you need legal advice (for example, 'How much maintenance should I pay?' or 'Do we need to sell the family home?'), and therefore a practising lawyer, as opposed to those issues where a divorce coach can be ideal (for example, 'My partner and I had a massive row today and I'm feeling really upset about it' or 'Can you help me do a first draft of a document for my solicitor to review?')

Parenting support

Co-parenting advice

Why?

If you have children, you are going to be co-parents for life. How you feel about your fellow co-parent on an adult, relationship level will no doubt be massively impacted by the divorce. But your aspirations for your children, the kind of childhood you want them to have and the kind of people you want them to grow up to be will all remain, despite the divorce. So you both need, for the sake of your children, to find a way to work together in the years to come, to support each other and have a co-parenting relationship which works.

Many parents feel instinctively gloomy, and often guilty, about getting divorced. Again, it comes down to stigma: there is a feeling that divorce in itself must be bad for children. We can't say this enough: *that is wrong*. What causes harm to children isn't divorce, it's conflict. And that can come from a bad marriage as well as from a bad divorce.

There is another, much more positive way to look at divorce: as an opportunity to redefine your relationship. Your intimate adult relationship is failing you and no longer makes you both happy. But your co-parenting relationship is separate, and this is an opportunity to make it work better for you both. Which is where a co-parenting expert can come in.

Cost?

Co-parenting experts used to work on hourly rates, but increasingly many are offering packages of support. At The Divorce Surgery we could see parents wanted help but didn't want open-ended fees or lengthy intervention, so we developed a Living Apart Parenting Together service. This combines legal and co-parenting expertise in a four-week process for a fixed fee. Whoever you use, be clear what your budget is before you start.

Joint?

Yes, although many services enable parents to have separate sessions if they prefer. For co-parenting to be effective, both parents ideally need to engage, as much of the work is learning how to communicate about your children in a way which is supportive and open, rather than pressing each other's buttons and (sometimes inadvertently) undermining each other.

Time-frame?

Again, it depends, but we'd usually say that if you get to the end of the third session and feel you're getting nowhere, then it's time to move on.

Benefits?

Over the years you will be faced with countless challenges (and joys) which your children thrust upon you. If each of these becomes a bone of contention between you, you will be faced with years, perhaps decades, of stress, and so will your children. And nobody wants to fall out. Your children certainly don't want you to fall out. So finding a way to work together is going to spare you, and your children, from the mental health impact of conflict. It will also save you a fortune in legal fees. Remember, too, that you are modelling for your children here – they are learning from you how to resolve conflict.

Pitfalls?

If there is a huge amount of mistrust between you, it can be difficult to jump straight into co-parenting work. For some couples, legal advice is a necessary precursor, because they need an understanding of what the law says and how a Family Judge might view their situation before they can start making any concessions or reaching agreements about their children. Getting legal advice first is fine, of course. But be careful. Don't let the process of obtaining advice drive you further apart. Don't start setting red lines ('I won't take less than 7 nights a fortnight'). Your children aren't commodities to be traded. So, do consider seeking joint, impartial legal advice. A co-parenting expert can then help you work together to improve your own communication and reach your own agreements which work for your children.

Financial expertise

Accountants

Why?

Your financial picture will form the backbone of the agreement you reach as to the division of your finances. So it's vital that it's accurate. But it's equally important that you both understand the basis for all the figures and have confidence in them. So, joint instructions (where you both instruct one financial expert to help you) are ideal, as you can both then work with the expert to understand the figures and reach a consensus on what there is to divide.

You will need to calculate your asset base net of tax (i.e. after any tax has been paid). An accountant can help you work out taxes relating to your income (particularly if you are self-employed or have deferred compensation), your assets (including properties, stocks and shares and other investments) and the way you run your financial life (for instance, if some of your assets are held abroad or in trust or corporate structures). You may have a shareholding in a business; if so, a specialist valuer may need to calculate not only the net value of your shareholding, but also your ability to draw down money from the business and the tax implications of doing so.

Cost?

If you are simply looking for a Capital Gains Tax calculation for a second home, or up-to-date tax returns to be prepared, there will be a one-off small fee. A business valuation will obviously be much more involved, but most experienced valuers will offer a fixed-fee quote based on the number of hours they expect the work to take.

Joint?

If you can, instruct an expert jointly. Not only is this the most cost-efficient way to operate, it also ensures the expert is providing an impartial opinion to you both. If you're going to reach a deal, it's crucially important that you both understand the basis for all the figures and have confidence in them. So joint instructions are ideal, as then you can both work with the expert to understand the figures and reach a consensus on what there is to divide.

Time-frame?

Agree this before you start, but unless your financial affairs are extremely complex, most accountants can produce the report you need in a matter of weeks.

Benefits?

It's boring, but it's essential. Neither of you wants to agree a financial deal and then find several months later that you are stung with a tax bill which you weren't expecting and which renders the agreement unfair.

Pitfalls?

Ensure you instruct someone who has experience in producing reports for divorce cases. If you are looking for a business valuation, this is a complex area and the basis of the instruction (i.e. the questions the expert is asked) is key. So you should ask a lawyer (either one you both share or the lawyers acting for each of you) to draft the letter of instruction, to ensure that the report produced covers all the bases and is done in a way which is compliant with Family Court procedure.

Independent financial advisers and wealth managers

Why?

As you will see in Step 6, a large part of the financial disclosure exercise is working out your future financial needs. Many of the financial agreements you reach will be dictated not by what the law says, but what is affordable in your circumstances. So, seeking advice at the earliest stage about each of your mortgage capacities and how much those mortgages will cost to service is vital.

Some couples are brilliant at budgeting and can easily produce a line by line analysis of what it costs them to live on a monthly basis. Most couples find the prospect of a budget extremely dull and can be prone to skip over it. But it's crucial. Financial advisers can analyse your past spending to produce a comprehensive budget, which can be an excellent starting-point.

You may be in a position where you are hoping not to pay maintenance to each other because you can each live off your own income and capital. Again, if capital is going to be a source of income to you, be clear about what is an achievable rate of return in the current financial markets. Cash-flow modelling will be hugely helpful for you both and any lawyers you instruct.

Cost?

This can be fixed fee or on an hourly rate. Always agree the fee and the scope of work before you commit.

Joint?

Not necessarily, although it can be helpful to at least have a joint meeting with the expert so you are both clear on the basis upon which the mortgage calculation or budget is being produced. Remember, if you both have confidence that the figures are correct and objective, you will be able to use them as the building blocks for any future agreement. If one of you feels a budget has been deliberately over-inflated for the benefit of the other, then frankly it isn't worth the paper it is written on.

Time-frame?

This depends on the complexity of the work, but we are talking weeks here. Remember mortgage offers expire, so factor that in to your timeline, as it's extremely frustrating to reach a deal only to find out that the mortgage you had been banking on is no longer available.

Benefits?

Mortgage capacity and budgets are often the foundations of a fair agreement. The best lawyer in the world cannot magic up a mortgage deal. So get this information early.

Pitfalls?

The biggest pitfall when it comes to budgets is trying to be tactical about it. Be realistic. It's not a wish-list. The best way to produce a budget is to use your bank statements showing your spending during the marriage. And of course that level of spending may well not be affordable now you are running two homes rather than one. If you can, crunch the numbers together so you're both clear about the monthly cost for each of you to run your respective homes and how that can be afforded.

Pensions on divorce experts and actuaries

Why?

Please don't gloss over this section! We know pensions are boring. But far too many couples (in particular far too many wives) fail to engage properly with what their pensions are worth and miss out. A study by the Nuffield Foundation in 2014[1] found that of the 369 Court files with a final financial remedy order studied, 80 per cent revealed at least one relevant pension and yet only 14 per cent contained a pension order. So many, many spouses had potentially been missing out on sharing the other's pension. This led to the establishment of the Pensions Advisory Group (PAG), an experienced group of senior Judges and practitioners from a diverse set of backgrounds. In July 2019 their final report was published.[2] It is the first guidance to assist professionals in how to approach pensions on divorce in the nearly 20 years that pension-sharing orders have been available. The link to the 176-page full report is in the endnotes and it is freely available online. It clearly cannot be summarized in a line(!), but the crucial takeaway is this: the 'value' of a pension that is produced by a pension scheme in its annual statement may well fall far short of the real value of the benefits that are paid out on retirement. Final salary schemes, public sector schemes and defined benefit schemes all have different and unique characteristics. So it is crucial for you both to obtain some expert input into what your pension benefits are worth and how you can share them fairly.

Cost?

Most pension on divorce experts and actuaries will do reports for a fixed fee.

Joint?

Yes, a joint instruction is the most cost-efficient way of getting the expertise. As with business valuations, the letter of instruction is vital, so do get legal advice if you can.

Time-frame?

This is often led by the time it takes for your pension providers to produce the information your pension expert needs, and some providers can be quite slow. Generally, you should be looking at six to eight weeks.

Benefits?

Spending a few thousand pounds on a pensions report is not the most exciting expenditure you'll ever make, but it could be the difference between a fair and comfortable retirement for you both or comfort for one and real financial hardship for the other. Plus, since the advent of the PAG report, most Family Judges simply won't convert financial agreements into Court Orders unless they are satisfied that pension rights have been properly and fairly considered.

Pitfalls?

Although we have put this ahead of legal advice, because we want you to start thinking about pensions at the earliest stage, you will benefit from legal advice before commissioning a pensions report. The reason for that is that you will need to agree the basis upon which the report is being prepared, or, to put it another way, what you are trying to achieve. Are you looking to equalize your pension incomes on retirement, so you are both in completely equivalent positions? Was some of the pension built up before the marriage or after you separated, and are you looking to take that out of the division? Is that realistic, given your respective needs in retirement and the other available resources? Are there particular tax or Lifetime Allowance implications which need to be taken into account and may require accountancy help? Once you have legal advice on all these issues, you can agree on the questions you would both like your chosen pensions expert to answer.

Legal advice

Sharing a lawyer

Why?

It's important, when choosing legal advice, to consider the end-game. Where is this all leading? Well, you want to end up with arrangements for your children and the division of your finances which are fair. The law is there to protect your respective rights and those of your children. A Family Judge will have to approve any financial deal you reach before it can be converted into a Court Order. That Judge won't be interested in what is the best outcome for one of you, but what is fair for your family as a whole. By sharing a lawyer who can advise you both impartially and objectively as to what is legally fair in your situation, you can work together, not against each other. At The Divorce Surgery we call this our 'One Couple One Lawyer' service. As at the time of writing, an increasing number of family lawyers are starting to offer their own versions of joint advice, recognizing that this is a service couples want. Do your homework and find out exactly what service is offered, and what it costs, before you commit to it.

Cost?

The Divorce Surgery operates on a fixed-fee model, so you know the total cost from the start. We did it that way because in our experience that's what the vast majority of divorcing couples want. And that's increasingly the way the market is going. So don't be afraid to push back on hourly rates and ask for a fixed-fee quote or shop around.

Joint?
Yes, save for the initial screening meetings to ensure you are both suitable, the entire process should be joint and transparent.

Time-frame?
It depends on how long the financial disclosure process takes, which depends on you, but once the financial disclosure is in, we will normally get couples to final advice within two to four weeks.

Benefits?
We are obviously biased here! Joint advice isn't right for every couple, and we talk more about this a little later in this step, but if you are suitable, it has huge benefits, enabling you to reach an agreement with less conflict, more quickly and for a fraction of the cost of two-lawyer models.

Pitfalls?
Your circumstances need to be suitable and you need to be emotionally ready. If you've only just found out that your former partner was having an affair, you aren't ready for legal advice, joint or otherwise. Also, coming to terms with the financial implications of running two households instead of one can be tough, and the right legal answer will probably leave you both feeling hard done by, so can sometimes be difficult to hear.

Two separate solicitors

Why?
Sometimes it's just not right for you to share a lawyer. You may be dealing with a former spouse who is abusive or hiding assets. You may want to start the process with your own solicitor and then move on to

joint advice. You need to do what is right for you and your family. It is vitally important to get legal advice, because divorce is a legal process, and you must ensure that you reach an outcome which is fair.

Cost?

Most solicitors charge on open-ended hourly rates. Some will offer fixed fees for bundles of work. Do set a budget and share that with your respective solicitors at the start of your working relationship. You should then all be on the same page as to how much you are expecting the work to cost, although be aware that the total fees will depend on how you negotiate and behave with each other. If the adversarial process escalates, there is little your respective solicitors can do to control the fees.

Joint?

No. At the time of writing, because of their conflict rules, most solicitors do not advise couples together, although this is evolving and many solicitors are looking at ways to offer a joint service in response to the huge client demand.

Time-frame?

This entirely depends on how your negotiations progress as a couple. You will spend the first few weeks largely communicating with your own solicitor about what you want to achieve, your family circumstances and your financial position, so they can help you prepare your case and decide how to pitch it. The amount of time you and your former spouse need to negotiate and reach a settlement after that really depends on the process you choose (*see further below*) and the two of you. A 2018 study by Aviva[3] found that the average divorce in the UK takes 14 months. If you end up litigating in the Family Court, it can take even longer.

Benefits?

We have each had the privilege, over many years as barristers, to work with truly fantastic solicitors. In many ways, family law is a vocation, and the people who are drawn to it undertake the work because they genuinely want to help people. The adversarial process undoubtedly makes it harder to keep things civilized, and so family solicitors have developed and routinely promote more amicable routes to settlement, including collaborative law, mediation and joint advice for at least part of the process. Many family solicitors are members of an organization called Resolution, which promotes a constructive approach to family issues.[4]

Pitfalls?

Choose your solicitor wisely. Make sure they share your values. It can be all too easy in a process you don't understand to delegate entirely to your lawyers. But you know your former spouse, and they don't. If the involvement of lawyers on each side is making things worse rather than better, take a step back and let them know. Remind yourselves of the end-game: reaching an agreement which is fair for you both. If that is being lost in the noise and your relationship is becoming more fractured as a result, consider a different approach.

Direct Access barristers

Why?

Barristers had always been a referral profession, meaning, in the past, that we could only be instructed by solicitors and not by members of the public directly. However, that all changed in 2004, when the Direct Access (or Public Access) scheme was launched. Now you can go straight to a barrister for advice or representation in Court. Many divorcing couples remain unaware of this as an option.

Cost?

Barristers usually charge on a fixed-fee basis for specific pieces for work, including preparation. Most barristers belong to a set of chambers which employ clerks to run their diaries, which includes quoting for the work and collecting fees. So if you are interested in exploring this as an option, you should be able to get a quote for the work before you commit.

Joint?

It can be. Barristers can advise a couple jointly as to what a Family Judge is likely to view as fair in their situation. Equally, barristers can advise one spouse or the other. It is up to each barrister to decide whether they think your case is suitable for Direct Access before they accept the instruction.

Time-frame?

Generally Direct Access is used to parachute in a barrister for a specific reason, for example representation at a Court hearing. So the time-frames are usually quite short – you will probably have a meeting with the barrister (called a conference) before the hearing to discuss your case and strategy and then they will attend the hearing with you and represent you. Some barristers do work alongside clients for a much longer time-frame, providing advice throughout the course of a case. It is important to explain to the clerks at the outset what your expectations are as to ongoing support, so they can find a barrister who is suitable (many simply have too many Court commitments to provide ongoing advice).

Benefits?

Direct Access is a fantastic and cost-effective resource if you are running your case without a solicitor (perhaps for cost reasons) but want ad hoc advice at different stages, or representation for a hearing. It can also be really useful when you need a second opinion, perhaps because you are anxious about the direction of travel your case is taking and want a fresh pair of eyes to look it over confidentially.

Pitfalls?

A Direct Access barrister isn't a substitute for a solicitor. Unless the barrister is specifically authorized by the Bar Council to conduct litigation (and many are not), they cannot run your case for you. Your barrister can advise you on the law, draft documents (including witness statements and letters) for you and represent you in Court or in settlement discussions. But if you are in Court proceedings, you will remain a 'litigant in person' and be responsible for filing necessary documents at Court and the general management of your case. The Bar Standards Board has produced guidance which explains how the Public Access scheme works and shows how members of the public can use it to instruct barristers directly.[5]

Non-legal advice

Mediators

Why?

The best way to resolve the legal consequences of a divorce, be they the finances or the arrangements for any children, is to agree them. A trained mediator can facilitate those discussions and get you both talking constructively about what the future will look like.

Cost?

Mediators usually charge on an hourly rate, which is generally much lower than a solicitor's hourly rate and can therefore be more cost-effective. At the time of writing, the government is offering a voucher scheme which provides a fixed contribution to the cost of mediation.

Joint?

Yes, although that doesn't mean you have to be in the same room. Mediators offer a range of options, including shuttle mediation, where you are in different rooms and the mediator moves between you, and hybrid mediation, where you are both accompanied by your solicitors.

Time-frame?

Each mediation session usually lasts around two hours. It can be hard to predict how many sessions you will need, but as a rule of thumb we normally say if you aren't finding progress is being made after three sessions, then try something different.

Benefits?

Mediation offers a supported way to get you talking. This is your life and your family up for discussion, so any process which kickstarts those discussions is a good start. If mediation is successful, you will save yourself a huge amount of legal fees in the long run and, even more importantly, you will have gained a valuable skill in resolving points of difference yourselves, and avoided the emotional fallout of the adversarial process.

Pitfalls?

Mediators cannot give legal advice. For many couples, this can be a real difficulty at the start of the process, because they don't know what their legal rights are and they don't know what a Court would consider to be fair in their situation. Our experience is that many couples benefit from joint legal advice before mediation starts, so they know the parameters of what is legally fair and achievable before they start negotiating.

Online divorce platforms

Why?

There are a variety of online platforms which, although not subject to regulation by the legal profession, offer assistance around the divorce process. Some give assistance simply with the divorce petition and others link you with divorce coaches who can support you through the process.

Cost?

Most online divorce platforms will offer fixed fees. But be careful to look into what you are paying for. As you will discover in this book, there is more to a divorce than a divorce petition, so if that is all you are getting for your money, it is not a full divorce service!

Joint?

It depends – some online platforms have divorce coaches attached to them who will work with couples together.

Time-frame?

Most will rely heavily on input from you, so the timescale will depend on the service being provided and how long you take to input the required information.

Benefits?

For very basic tasks, where you feel confident you can proceed without legal advice, these can be cost-effective. If the service links you up with a divorce coach, then it will have all the benefits we have already described and can be really valuable.

Pitfalls?

You need to investigate exactly what the service is that you are paying for and who is undertaking it. Do you need a qualified lawyer to advise you, who will be regulated by the Bar Standards Board (for barristers) or the Solicitors Regulatory Authority (for solicitors)? A divorce is, for many people, the most significant financial settlement they will make in their lifetime. Be very wary of concluding a deal without getting some legal advice, as once a Court Order is made, it is very difficult to undo.

How do these all fit together?

Please don't be bamboozled by all these options. You won't need anything like all of them! Remember, options are good. For far too long separating couples have been led to believe their only choices are two separate solicitors or one mediator. In fact, you have a rich tapestry of interconnecting options at your disposal.

Let's look at some case studies to see how they all fit together.

MARK AND DAVID

We met Mark and David at the start of this step. Despite being in a fractious place, they decide to secure some joint legal advice.

Both are reassured that the Court will want to consider all their circumstances. They each have valid points to make. The first stage is to get their financial disclosure together.

With the help of their joint lawyer, they jointly instruct an accountant to prepare a valuation of Mark's shareholding in his business (now, at the time of the separation and when they started living together) and also look at how liquid the company is (i.e. the extent to which Mark would be able to draw down capital from the business) and the tax consequences of this.

Mark and David also instruct a pensions on divorce expert to prepare a pension-sharing report in order for them to understand how they might fairly, and tax efficiently, share the pensions that were built up during the marriage, but exclude those that were built up before they started living together.

Mark and David have each prepared separate budgets, but they cannot agree on them. David feels that Mark's is excessively frugal and does not reflect the way they lived when they were together. Mark thinks David's is deliberately over-inflated. They both agree to appoint a shared budgeting expert who will go through their bank statements and produce an impartial summary of how they spent their money during their marriage.

Once all the financial information has been collated, Mark and David return for further joint legal advice.

Neither is completely happy with the advice – David is feeling short-changed and Mark worries the settlement is too generous – so they take their written advice to separate solicitors, who analyse it from each of their perspectives and conclude it is fair, but come up with tweaks which their respective clients find more palatable. There follows six weeks of solicitor negotiation by email, and a settlement is reached.

MARY AND GEOFF

You may remember Mary and Geoff from Step 1. After 30 years of marriage, Mary discovered Geoff was having an affair when she saw a WhatsApp message come up on his mobile phone. Her first instinct was to call a solicitor and start divorce proceedings, but her sister held her back.

Instead, Mary approached a divorce coach. She told Geoff and they agreed not to take any legal steps for three months. They also agreed that it was too difficult to continue living together. Fortunately, they were in a financial position that allowed Geoff to rent a nice property nearby. They kept all their other financial arrangements the same and continued to use the joint account so that they remained transparent about their spending.

Mary's divorce coach suggested that they both try separation counselling to talk about their marriage and its legacy. Both found this hard, but ultimately quite cathartic. With a professional in the room, Mary felt better able to express her horror at Geoff's betrayal and how it made her feel that the last 30 years had been a waste of her life. What had it all been for? Geoff was able, for the first time, to express his shame about how the marriage had ended, but also the extreme loneliness he had felt for the past five years. Whilst not understanding each other, Mary and Geoff had at least begun to see the other's perspective and acknowledge that their marriage had achieved many wonderful things. Both felt relieved that they could choose a narrative around divorce which was amicable, so they didn't have to keep reliving how it ended.

When the time came for legal advice, Geoff was extremely anxious that the work of their separation counsellor could be undone by an adversarial process. They started with mediation, but Mary didn't feel confident enough about their financial situation, and her divorce coach, although supportive, was not legally trained.

Mary therefore engaged a solicitor to advise her between mediation sessions. Although this was useful for her, Geoff felt out of the loop and was anxious about Mary possibly misrepresenting what her solicitor had said. Mary's solicitor, and the mediator, suggested they take some joint legal advice, as they were becoming entrenched in their respective positions, particularly regarding the amount of maintenance Mary should receive and for how long.

At the joint advice session, they were advised about how a Court would view maintenance and the bracket of likely outcomes. They felt much closer to a resolution, but wanted to explore capitalizing maintenance. They jointly instructed a financial planner to do some cash-flow modelling for them and explore likely rates of return.

They had one final mediation session and settled. Mary's solicitor then drafted a Court Order reflecting their agreement.

'SO, WHAT ARE OUR OPTIONS?'

As you decide the types of professional you want to engage, it's worth thinking about how this ties in with the process of reaching agreement. The vast majority of separating couples don't agree about every aspect of their divorce. That is entirely normal. So you need to decide, as early as you can, on a process by which agreement can be reached. Other couples do agree on everything, but need their financial agreement ratified by a Family Judge for it to be binding. So they need to know if their agreement is one a Family Judge will view as fair.[6]

Your routes to settlement divide into two camps: those in which you work together to reach an agreement; and those in which you work against each other, putting forward two competing arguments and delegating the job of choosing between you to a third party.

Most couples will want to start, for obvious reasons, in the 'working together' category. As you can imagine, that's what we suggest.

Working together

'Working together' in the context of divorce is relatively new. As we discussed in the last step, the Family Justice system is in crisis, reidentifying its role and working out how it should be helping divorcing families. But what this means for you, now, is that not all family law professionals will necessarily be familiar with all the processes that are now available. Which means they will steer you to the ones they know. So it is vital that you are aware of the many different services that are now emerging, so you can choose the divorce you want.

Working separately

Of course there are situations where working together is simply not possible, nor would we recommend it, for instance:

- If there is an abuse dynamic between you. If you don't feel safe in your relationship and wouldn't feel safe in a joint process, you should urgently seek legal advice from a solicitor and consider contacting the police and social services. The law is there to protect you and your family as a whole. Please use it.
- If you think your former partner is going to be fundamentally dishonest about finances. This isn't the same as wanting different outcomes. It isn't dishonest to have drastically opposing views as to what your monthly household budgets should be, for instance. But if you believe your former partner has started or may begin a campaign to hide assets, for example by moving them off-shore into corporate or trust structures, rather than disclose them, you should urgently seek independent legal advice from a solicitor who has experience in tracing assets across multiple jurisdictions. This is a specialist field, so do ask about their track record. If it (happily) transpires that your fears were unfounded, you can always begin a joint process then.
- If you have links with countries outside England and Wales such that you may want to divorce in another country, then again you should seek urgent legal advice from a solicitor. Time is of the absolute essence here. This is an occasion when you really can't let each other know your plans and you will need to take unilateral action. Different countries have radically different laws on divorce, which could be hugely disadvantageous to one or the other of you. If you think this scenario may apply to you, take urgent advice, on your own, from a solicitor who has experience in international family law. Again, this is a highly specialist area, so ensure the solicitor you choose can give you examples of cases they have successfully navigated where this issue has arisen. And don't be afraid that this early disagreement will then lead to further fallout – on the contrary. We deal with many couples who start their case with a disagreement about which country is the right one to deal with their divorce, but then, once that issue is resolved, come back to us to deal with their finances and children's arrangements together.

Remember that even if you start in adversarial proceedings about one issue, you can move back into a joint process to resolve other aspects of your divorce, and vice versa.

In the Family Solutions Group report 'What About Me',[7] prepared by a multi-disciplinary group of experienced family professionals and endorsed by the President of the Family Division, divorce processes were divided into those that help couples work together and those that set them against each other. We have used that idea to create the table below, but the report itself is freely available on the internet and worth a read if you're really getting into this/can stomach 164 pages of legal chat!

Process	Working together or working apart?
Resolve issues together around the kitchen table with no professional help	Together
Jointly instruct a non-legal professional (e.g. accountant or co-parenting expert)	Together
Jointly instruct a divorce coach or counsellor	Together
Mediation	Together
Jointly instruct one lawyer (e.g. One Couple One Lawyer services, The Divorce Surgery)	Together
Shuttle mediation (in separate rooms/ online meetings so no contact with each other)	Together
Hybrid mediation (each side supported by their own solicitor and other professionals)	Together but legal advice is not shared with each other
Collaborative law (you each have solicitors but contract with your solicitors and each other not to go to court)	Together but separate legal advice throughout

Early Neutral Evaluation (ENE) (a senior barrister or solicitor is instructed by both of you to provide their view as to what is fair. Normally you will each be instructing separate solicitors by this point)	Together but the context is that you will each have had separate legal advice for some time and prepared your case separately so you need to be careful not to see each other as being in different 'camps'
Round Table Meeting (where each of you attends a meeting with your separate solicitors and sometimes also barristers in an attempt to negotiate a settlement)	Apart. The reality here is that by this point you will have each spent many months preparing your case in separate legal silos. Obviously this is far better than the more adversarial processes below, but there will still be strong elements of a two sided-process.
Each instruct separate solicitors or direct access barristers who settle your case in correspondence without going to court	Apart and separate legal advice throughout. Because you don't know the legal advice the other receives, you can each separately still feel the outcome was 'unfair'.
MedArb (this is a process by which you start with mediation and commit that the issues you cannot agree will be referred to an arbitrator to resolve)	Together and Apart – if you do not agree, an outcome will be imposed on you by an experienced barrister or solicitor acting as an arbitrator.
Arbitration	Apart – arbitration has many advantages compared to court: it is quicker, you can choose your judge and in most cases it will be more cost-efficient because you will not be waiting months for a hearing date. But in terms of how it feels for divorcing couples, it is very similar to court. You will each be represented by barristers and solicitors and cross-examined by the 'other side'. So the emotional fallout can be tough.

Court proceedings	Apart. It is worth bearing in mind that even in the court process the Family Judge will, at every stage, be encouraging you to broker a settlement. In financial cases there is always a settlement hearing (known as a Financial Dispute Remedy hearing or FDR) at which a judge will tell you what he/she believes the outcome should be so you can try to settle. Your solicitors can also arrange private FDRs, where you jointly instruct a senior barrister or solicitor to perform the role of a judge. It is of course far better to settle than go to trial, but in terms of the impact on your mental health, your relationship with each other and the wider family, to a large extent the damage has been done. You will have been in conflict for many months, sometimes only corresponding through solicitors, which takes a heavy emotional and financial toll.

AMY AND ADRIAN

Amy and Adrian have been separated for five years. They have one son, TJ, who is now 8 years old, and was 3 when they separated.

They had a very fractious break-up. The birth of TJ, whilst joyful, put a huge strain on the couple. Hard choices were made about balancing their work commitments, childcare, nurseries and priorities, compounded by lack of sleep. As they emerged from the fog, Amy realized she just didn't want to be married to Adrian any more.

One day when Adrian was at work, Amy packed her bags, collected TJ from nursery and took him to stay with her mother. She really only planned to go for a couple of days to clear her head. But she didn't tell Adrian, which she would now acknowledge was a huge mistake. That one lapse in communication had a snowball effect which triggered many months of litigation.

Adrian returned home from work and his wife and son had gone. He couldn't get through to Amy on her mobile. He was in a state of high panic when he called the police and a family solicitor.

Emergency Court proceedings followed, on the basis that TJ needed to be located, as Amy had abducted him. Amy and her mother were visited by the police to ensure TJ was safe, which Amy found mortifying. Adrian felt bereft in the family home alone and desperately missed his son. Amy felt he had completely over-reacted. Already the mistrust was building. Neither felt able simply to pick up the phone and talk to the other. Angry texts were exchanged.

Amy instructed her own solicitor. Given the state of their relationship, it seemed inconceivable that she could move back into the family home with Adrian. But they couldn't afford both the mortgage and a rental property. Amy suggested Adrian move out so that she and TJ could move back in. But where was he to go? He said he couldn't afford to move out until they had agreed how their finances were to be divided and housing needs met. The effect was that Amy and TJ remained living with her mother, a three-hour drive away from Adrian. Amy could work remotely, so there was no imperative for her to return.

Adrian's time with TJ was very limited. For Amy, this was a logistics issue to do with the drive time, but Adrian started to question her motives. Was this move to her mother's driven by a desire to marginalize him from TJ's life? Was he losing his son? This state of fear heightened the litigation. Adrian changed his position. He was no longer seeking a shared care arrangement for TJ, but arguing that Amy was attempting to remove him from TJ's life. Given she could no longer be trusted to promote his role as TJ's father, he felt TJ should be based with him, not his mother.

This had now become a fight for TJ. Legal fees escalated. There was a small amount of equity in the family home and they borrowed against it to pay the legal fees. Through the months that followed, letters and witness statements were drafted. As time went on and mistrust continued to build, attitudes hardened. Amy and Adrian were now unrecognizable from the parents they had been during the marriage. Direct communication broke down and they found themselves asking their solicitors to check emails to each other before they sent them, in case they had said something that could later be used against them in Court.

TJ was impacted by the conflict. He witnessed his parents' animosity at handovers and cried every time he had to go, begging Amy not to take him. She believed this was because he didn't want to see his father and didn't enjoy his time with him. But what she didn't see was that 5 minutes after she'd left he'd be laughing and happy in his father's car. What distressed TJ was being around his parents' hostility to each other.

Eventually, 20 months later, the litigation ended. An order was made for shared care. Nobody 'won'. The lawyers all went away. Amy and Adrian were emotionally and financially decimated. What now? From corresponding only with the help of their solicitors, they suddenly had to email and text each other direct. It was a huge adjustment, which initially they simply could not overcome. At points Amy wanted to change the arrangements, and more Court proceedings were threatened, but in reality neither could face it again.

Eventually, they both agreed to access joint co-parenting advice. TJ was a sensitive boy and his parents were both worried that if they didn't do something their conflict would cause long-term damage to him. They were given techniques for listening to each other and co-parenting, and understood that a failure in communication had been what had let them down. Their relationship remains fragile, but functions.

Perhaps it was always going to be that journey for Amy and Adrian, but imagine if they'd accessed emotional and co-parenting support *before* Amy left. Frankly, if they'd just talked to each other and made a plan, could that have saved them, and TJ, the many months of stress that followed?

Right, we've set out all the options. Now it's time to agree on a divorce plan which works for your family.

OVER TO YOU ...

Making your divorce plan

Ideally we would like you to do this together, unless it's clear that one of you needs to take urgent legal advice on your own.

You need to make an initial plan which covers what professional support you need, in what order, how long it should all take and what your overall budget is going to be.

So, taking each point in turn:

Emotional

- Do you need emotional support on your own?
- Do you need support together to help you both talk through the separation?
- If you have children, do you need support in telling them about your decision to separate? Are you still able to talk about the children? Do they need support themselves?

Financial

- Do you understand your finances? Would you like support to go through them?
- Are there aspects to your financial situation which will need expert input – pensions, tax, business valuations?
- Do you feel confident in preparing a budget? Can you agree what your spending was during the marriage?

Legal

- Would you like joint or separate legal advice? (Remember, you can start with one and move to the other.)

- Do you have a reason for urgent legal advice (for example, if you don't feel safe or fear your former partner may be planning to hide assets from you)? If so, prioritize seeing a solicitor above everything else.
- In what order do you need the help?
  » List the most pressing issues in order of priority (you are likely to see that the legal issues are medium term but not immediate priorities).
- How much time are you going to allocate for each stage?
  » For each stage, set out how many weeks or sessions you feel is proportionate. Then reach out to the various professionals and see what they say is achievable. The key benefit to making an informed plan is that you can explain your rationale and hopefully from the start you can all be working to the same achievable aim.
- How much do you want to spend?
  » This is crucial. Most divorcing couples simply start the process with no idea how long it will take or how much it will cost. You would never do that for any other significant financial expenditure (imagine starting a kitchen extension without a total budget), so don't do it here.
  » Allocate budgets to each item of professional expenditure.
  » Then start getting quotes in. Don't be afraid, at every stage, to ask for a fixed-fee quote. Be clear what your total budget is for the service. Solicitors can, for instance, come off the record for periods of time as a way of helping you save money.

That's it. Well done. We hope that making a plan will help you feel more in control. This is *your* divorce, and it's going to be so much easier to navigate if you both keep hold of the reins.

When you're ready, it's time for the next step, which is engaging with some of the short-term plans you'll need to make. We're here to guide you through it.

STEP 4

||||||||||||||||||||||||||||||||||||||||||||||||||||||||||||||||||||||||||||||

MAKING SHORT-TERM PLANS

||||||||||||||||||||||||||||||||||||||||||||||||||||||||||||||||||||||||||||||

'Should we start changing things right away?
Who's moving out?
Should we get divorced?'

So now you know what you want to achieve and what options are available to help you get there. You may already have some ideas about what support you'll need. Maybe you're already accessing it … If so, brilliant – you're proceeding fast. If not, take your time and don't worry. You'll make better decisions in the long run if you've prepared the ground thoroughly and feel calm, supported and ready. This can all wait.

However, at some point, when the time is right, you'll need to start thinking about some practicalities: the fundamental, long-term stuff about money and, if you have them, the kids. Not just yet. But life goes on and that means decisions need taking day to day about a variety of things both to do with the process of separating itself and simply daily living. Who's paying the gas bill? Who's picking the kids up from karate on Wednesday?

Of course not all short-term decisions are equally momentous. Whether you should cancel next summer's family holiday or not is unlikely to be a critical issue. But should you take that promotion you've just been offered, even though you'll have to move to a different part of the country? Is your friend really right when he says you shouldn't move out of the family home, because if you do you seriously weaken your negotiating power when it comes to the finances? Should you tell the children about your new relationship, and if so, what you should tell them and how? Should you repay your parents that money they lent you ten years ago to fund the extension? Should you agree equal care of the children right away? Or ever?

You cannot realistically hope to take decisions like these from a short-term perspective. You will need some understanding of where the train is headed before you leave the station. This is crucial to building confidence – both your own and your confidence in each other's commitment to working together through this process.

So this step is going to focus on introducing you to the basic legal landscape surrounding:

- your relationship status and what's going to happen next, including a discussion of 'no-fault divorce'
- your money
- your children, if you have them

Then we'll circle back to some of the more common short-term issues that tend to arise.

THE LEGAL LANDSCAPE

If you'll excuse the disclaimer, what follows is an introduction – it is not and never can be a substitute for legal and other relevant professional advice tailored to your specific circumstances. But our hope is it will empower you with much more knowledge than you otherwise would have, so you can lead discussions about the next steps, rather than let the divorce be something that happens to you.

Your relationship status

You've decided to move on from your current relationship, but what now? At the risk of stating the obvious, whether you are married or not makes a big difference.

'We're married'

If you are divorcing, you are changing your relationship status from 'married' to 'divorced'. There are legal and often also financial and tax consequences that flow from that change of status, but you can leave those to one side for the moment (we'll come back to these shortly).

So the first question, if you are married but separating, is:

Do you want to get divorced?

Some couples don't know at first. Perhaps you just want to cement your separation, to take things slowly and to deal with the formalities later, as and when the time feels right. Maybe you're just starting a new job, or have a child who is about to start a new school. Life doesn't stop because of divorce. A careful consideration of timing is key.

We see lots of couples for whom the very idea of divorcing, with all the baggage it brings, is just too much at this stage. Perhaps one or both of you has a religious objection. That's completely fine – there is much that can be done to prepare for the future without formally divorcing. Whether to divorce or not is an intensely personal decision which is nothing whatsoever to do with your lawyers or anyone else. Take your time to consider what you really want, without making assumptions as to what is 'normal'. Ignore the outside noise as much as you can.

This may be the very last thing on your mind as you process the ending of your current relationship, but it's worth bearing in mind that you *cannot* remarry unless you have first divorced.[1] Therefore if remarriage is on the cards for either of you, there will have to be a divorce at some point.

'What actually is a divorce and how do I get one?'

To reiterate, we're only talking about divorce itself here. We'll come on to the potentially more complex issues of money and children in a moment.

First up, there is no such thing as a 'quickie divorce', whether you're rich and famous, destitute or somewhere in between. In principle at least, the position has always been that all uncontested divorces should take the same time to process. No short cuts.

On the other hand, the good news is that the process in England and Wales has very recently become considerably more humane (although not necessarily quicker), with the arrival, as of 6 April 2022, of the new and long-awaited 'no-fault divorce' rules.[2]

Many of you may have already begun the process under the previous divorce rules. If so, and for those of you who want to understand why no-fault divorce is likely to be an improvement, it is important to know a bit about the system we are leaving behind.

The old system for getting a divorce – 'conduct-based divorce'

To obtain a divorce in England and Wales, the parties had to have been married for at least one year.

MARY AND GEOFF

Under this system, if Mary (from Step 3) wishes to divorce Geoff, she will have to prove that the 'marriage has broken down irretrievably', for one of five reasons:

- Geoff committed adultery and, as such, Mary finds it intolerable to live with him.
- Geoff behaved in such a way that Mary could not reasonably be expected to live with him (commonly known as 'unreasonable behaviour' by family lawyers).
- Geoff has 'deserted' (i.e. abandoned) Mary for at least two continuous years.
- Mary and Geoff have been separated for at least two years *and* Geoff consents to a divorce.
- Mary and Geoff have been separated for at least five years, regardless of whether Geoff consents.

But Mary and Geoff are making good progress towards understanding the reasons why their marriage has ended. Mary is uncomfortable making use of any of the first three grounds whilst their relationship remains so delicate. Geoff wholeheartedly agrees. But neither wants to wait a minimum of two years following their separation. What are they to do?

The conventional solution to Mary and Geoff's problem has been to proceed on the basis of unreasonable behaviour, but the shortcomings of this were brutally exposed in a case that went all the way to the Supreme Court:

OWENS V OWENS [2018]

Mr and Mrs Owens married in 1978. When Mrs Owens petitioned for divorce in May 2015, she was 68 and Mr Owens was 80. The parties were already living separately.

Mrs Owens argued that she was entitled to a divorce on the basis of what she alleged was Mr Owens' unreasonable behaviour. Examples of this were that Mr Owens 'had prioritized his work over their life at home; that his treatment of her had lacked love or affection; that he had often been moody and argumentative; that he had disparaged her in front of others; and that as a result she had felt unhappy, unappreciated, upset and embarrassed and had over many years grown apart from him.'

Mr Owens disagreed. He denied that the marriage had irretrievably broken down.

The Court agreed with him and as result Mrs Owens' petition was dismissed.

Because Mr Owens did not consent to divorce, and none of the other available grounds for a divorce were made out, she was forced to remain married to him for five years from the date of their separation, even though their marriage had clearly broken down.

Divorcing couples and family lawyers had been bemoaning this state of affairs for literally decades before the Owens' case hit the headlines. The outcry that followed put the issue at the forefront of public consciousness: in the current day and age, how can it be right for one spouse to be trapped in a marriage? And at last the cavalry has arrived in the form of no-fault divorce, thanks to the Divorce, Dissolution and Separation Act 2020, in operation from April 2022.

The new system: No-fault divorce in England and Wales

No-fault divorce removes the focus on one party's conduct as a factor which is relevant to the divorce. No one has to prove anything – adultery, desertion or unreasonable behaviour. Or wait two or five years to proceed.

Instead, a spouse, or both spouses acting jointly if they agree, will simply have to *notify* the Court that the marriage has broken down irretrievably. *It will not be possible to contest the divorce.*

There will be a new minimum period of 20 weeks from the start of proceedings to the date when the Court can make a Conditional Order. Six weeks after that, the Court can conclude matters by making a Divorce Order.

Why is this better?

Apart from the obvious point that under the new regime no one will fall into the same trap as Mrs Owens, it is, above all, kinder.

The problem that family lawyers, commentators and Judges have long identified is that if you require parties to make allegations at the point of separation, then you are making their future relationships that much harder. This can have a material impact when it comes to discussions about money and children. If you have been obliged to focus on your spouse's behaviour as the reason why you can no longer remain married, do you think that will help or hinder discussions about the arrangements for caring for your children, for example? This is almost exactly what the Supreme Court itself said in *Owens v Owens*:

> Family lawyers are well aware of the damage caused by the requirement under the current law that, at the very start of proceedings based on the sub-section, one spouse must make allegations of behaviour against the other. Such allegations often inflame their relationship, to the prejudice of any amicable resolution of the ensuing financial issues and to the disadvantage of any children.[3]

No-fault divorce removes the confrontational aspect, and so creates better conditions for amicable discussions. Now, Mary and Geoff can issue a joint application to the Court, providing notification that they wish to divorce. There is no requirement for any focus on Geoff's conduct.

'We aren't married'

This is much simpler. The fundamental point to note here is that if you are unmarried, the law does not require you to do anything formally to dissolve your relationship.

It doesn't matter if you have been with your partner for 2 months or 20 years, whether you cohabit or not, whether you have children together or not, whether you have taken each other's last name or not, or whether you own property together or not. There *may* be consequences if you receive state benefits, in relation to tax and of course in respect to your children if you have them. But as far as simply ending the relationship is concerned, no further action is needed.

What about 'common law marriage', we hear you say? Cue much sighing and gnashing of teeth from the lawyers in the room. Try googling 'the myth of common law marriage' and you will see pages and pages of blogs written by family lawyers (including ourselves) earnestly seeking to debunk this enduring misunderstanding.

But without success, apparently. The idea of common law marriage is so deeply embedded in our culture that according to a 2019 study by the National Centre for Social Research,[4] nearly half of us in England and Wales still wrongly believe that unmarried couples who cohabit have a common law marriage, a figure largely unchanged since 2005. This is despite an enormous increase in the number of cohabiting couples during that period. Bizarrely, even half of *married* couples (49 per cent) believe in common law marriage.

Of course the reasons for the belief are entirely understandable. How can it be right that a couple can spend 20 years together, potentially have a family together, make all of the emotional, financial and practical sacrifices of marriage, and yet be able to walk away without any obligations whatsoever to each other? The lack of legal protection for cohabiting but unmarried couples is seen by many family lawyers as a great injustice. But it requires Parliament to step in and make new law; until it does so, the Courts remain powerless.

So, it is vital to understand *there is no such thing as common law marriage in England and Wales. Full stop.*

Your money

Again, very different rules apply, depending on whether you are married or not. This can be a huge problem for separating cohabitees, as we shall see, and is likely to become an ever bigger problem for us all as time passes: according to the Office for National Statistics, the total number of cohabiting couples in the UK has increased from around 1.5 million in 1996 to around 3.4 million in 2020, an increase of 127 per cent.[5]

Unless and until there is a change in the law, there will continue to be a gulf between the financial claims able to be made by married and unmarried couples.

'We're married'

Bear in mind that getting divorced does *not* automatically mean your finances will be resolved. Separate legal proceedings are required for each process. Dealing with the money is known as 'financial remedy proceedings'. You will have to ask the Court (and pay an application fee), if you want the Court to deal with finances.

If you do, the main point to note is that the Family Court continues to exercise a closely supervisory role when it comes to the financial arrangements between separating spouses.

As we have already seen, if you want a fully binding financial deal between you, you will have to get the Court to approve it. But before it will do that, the Court will have to be satisfied that it is fair to each of you. Courts can and do refuse to approve settlements that fail this basic test.

What can the Court do?

The Court has the power to redistribute your property between you when you separate. It does not necessarily matter whether, for example, the property is owned jointly or is only in the name of one of you. We'll look at this in more detail in Step 8, but for now be aware that the Court can make orders:

- for spousal maintenance, being payments, usually on a monthly basis, to provide a regular income to the other spouse to meet their day-to-day needs. These can either be for a defined period of time, or in rare cases even until one of you dies (called a 'joint lives' order)
- for school fees
- for the payment of capital lump sums. A lump sum is a one-off payment of a defined amount of money. The Court can order more than one lump sum.
- transferring ownership of property (houses, cars, savings, policies, belongings, company shareholdings and so on)
- for child maintenance, but only in certain circumstances[6]
- dividing up your pensions
- varying any relevant pre- or post-nuptial settlements (for example, certain trust funds)

All you need to know for now is that the Family Court has very wide powers indeed to do what it considers fair. It can and routinely does make orders transferring one party's property to the other, with or without that party's agreement.

'If we think we're going to want the Court to sort out our finances, do we also need to get divorced?'

The short answer is yes, if you want a binding Court Order. The Court's powers to make orders in relation to your *finances* only arise at all if you have also reached a certain stage in your *divorce* proceedings (Decree Nisi under the old rules, or Conditional Order under the new no-fault divorce rules).

This is worth bearing in mind at an early stage, given that it can take some time to process the divorce. Many couples choose, for legal reasons, to start divorce proceedings, negotiate a financial settlement whilst awaiting their Conditional Order, and then finalize the finances before returning to finish off the divorce afterwards.

A particular point to watch out for is that there may be detrimental financial consequences in applying for the final Divorce Order (or Decree Absolute under the old rules) before you have a Court Order in relation to the division of your finances, in particular with regards to your ability to claim pension benefits if one of you were to die before your financial agreement is approved, your rights to occupy the family home if it is legally held in the name of the other spouse, and also in relation to tax. Equally you need to be careful to ensure, if you are intending to share a pension, to wait 28 days from the date the financial order is approved before applying for the Divorce Order, so that the pension sharing order can take immediate effect on pronouncement of the Divorce Order and preserve death benefits in the meantime. It is always worth taking legal advice on these small (but very important) timing points. The process looks like this:

ALVARO AND PAMELA

Alvaro and Pamela issue divorce proceedings under the no-fault divorce rules. As the clock starts to tick on the 20-week statute-imposed time for reflection, they simultaneously begin to consider financial issues and negotiate a financial settlement.

- After 20 weeks, they obtain a Conditional Order in the divorce proceedings, but take no further steps afterwards.
- They submit a financial consent order to the Family Court for approval.
- The Family Court approves the financial consent order.

- They apply to finalize the divorce and obtain a Divorce Order. (This must be a minimum of six weeks after the Conditional Order.)

llllllllllllllllllllllllllllllllllllllllllllllllllllllllllllllllllllllllllllllllllllllllllllllllllllllllllllllllllllllllllll

'So, can we resolve our finances without getting divorced or getting a Court Order?'

Broadly, also yes. You don't have to have your financial settlement approved by the Court and in recent years 'separation agreements' have become increasingly popular as an alternative. A separation agreement is a formal document recording your settlement, the difference being it is not approved by a Court and is not a Court Order.

Whilst properly drawn up and negotiated separation agreements can often do the job, they are not binding in the sense that a Court Order is and have some limitations, for example they cannot include a pension sharing order. If one of you decided in the future that the agreement was no longer suitable, and there was subsequent litigation, a Court would be duty bound to consider whether the separation agreement provided for a fair outcome at the present time, and if it did not, could impose different arrangements. For many, therefore, obtaining a binding financial consent order from the Court will be the most attractive option to ensure finality.

'Do I have to sort out the finances? It sounds complicated and I'm not sure I can face it'

Not at all. You don't have to do anything. But if you have already decided that you want to *divorce*, there can be good reasons to sort out your financial issues at the same time, essentially because your financial claims against each other arising out of marriage will remain 'open' even *after* you have divorced, until such time as a Court deals with them.

This can have very dramatic consequences:

VINCE V WYATT [2015]

Dale Vince and Kathleen Wyatt were married in 1981. Ms Wyatt had a daughter from a previous relationship and in 1983 the parties had a son together.

During the marriage, the family was of very modest means, living mainly off state benefits. In 1984, the couple separated. Ms Wyatt cared for the children without financial support from Mr Vince, who could not afford to make payments.

They divorced in 1992 and pursued their lives independently afterwards. However, their financial claims against each other were not (the Court found) dealt with at the time of the divorce.

Ms Wyatt went on to have two further children, whereas Mr Vince founded a green energy business which went on to become extraordinarily successful, with an estimated value of £57m by the time of the Court hearing in 2011, 19 years after their divorce was finalized, when Ms Wyatt asked the Court for financial help from Mr Vince.

After many years of arguing in the Courts, the case reached the Supreme Court in 2015. In the end, Mr Vince ended up paying a lump sum of more than £600,000 to meet the claim against him – not much in the context of his overall wealth, and far less than Ms Wyatt had previously argued for, but significant nonetheless. Mr Vince also had not only to fund his own legal fees, but also contribute to Ms Wyatt's, as she could not pay her own.

At the time of their separation, neither party could have predicted the incredible financial resources that Mr Vince would go on to acquire. Had they resolved their financial issues at that point, there would have been nothing left for them to argue about.

Another major consideration when it comes to decisions about timing is tax. The treatment of Capital Gains Tax in particular will depend on how long ago you separated and whether you are still in the tax year of separation when you move assets between you, amongst other things. In short, you will want to ensure you structure any financial settlement and timetable any transfers of assets tax-efficiently. You should always take specialist tax advice if you have significant financial resources to divide.

It's crucially important to be aware that if you remarry this will have a very significant impact on your legal entitlement to make financial claims arising from your former marriage. So if you intend to remarry, you really must sort your finances out first.

'We aren't married'

Completely different rules apply when it comes to resolving financial issues between unmarried couples. However, it depends to some extent on whether you have children together.

'What can the Court do if we don't have children together?'

If you were in an unmarried relationship without children, the stark and unfortunate reality is you have *no* family law rights to bring financial claims against each other, other than on a very limited basis indeed (relating to the occupation of any property you may share). Once again, it makes no difference how long your relationship lasted. You cannot bring a claim for maintenance, lump sums, or a share of each other's pensions. You cannot ask the Court to transfer your former partner's assets to you. In summary, yours and your former partner's separate and individual property remains just that – separate and individual.

What you can do is ask the Court to divide up property in a way that reflects what was already intended between you. Of course, in the fog of separation you may disagree over what was intended ... This is a highly fact-specific and difficult area of law and you should always seek specialist legal advice if you think this applies to you.

'What if we've had children together?'

Then the Court has powers similar to, but not as wide as, those it would have if you were married (*see above*), at least until your children turn 18, or later if they are continuing in further education and in certain other circumstances.

It can make orders:

- for the payment of capital lump sums from one of you to the other, if this is justified by the needs of your children
- providing for children to be housed until a defined point in the future. But importantly, any property provided in this way is not provided *outright*. It will revert back to the parent providing it when it is no longer needed by your children.
- for child maintenance, but only in certain circumstances where the Child Maintenance Service cannot deal with it

The crucial difference from 'married cases' is that the Court makes orders *for the benefit of the children* and not simply because it is *fair* to do so in view of the length of the relationship and so on. So if orders aren't required to meet a child's needs (or those of parents caring for their children), they will not be made at all.

Let's consider what all these confusing differences look like in practice:

NICO AND ERIN

Nico and Erin married in 1994, when they were both 26, and have two children together, now aged 24 and 22.

During the marriage, Nico worked as an engineer on oil rigs and spent large amounts of time overseas. He is now exclusively UK-based and is in a management position earning £80,000 gross pa.

Erin worked part time as a school teacher, fitting her employment around child-caring responsibilities. She still works part time, earning £15,000 gross pa.

Broadly, Nico was the 'breadwinner' and Erin the 'homemaker'. Each considers they worked hard in their respective roles during the marriage. Nico handled the finances throughout and considers that he 'bought' the family home, which is in his name, and has paid the mortgage throughout.

The parties' relationship faded whilst the children were at university and they separated shortly after the younger child moved out.

The couple, now in their early fifties, are financially comfortable:

- Their home is worth £550,000 with a mortgage of only £50,000.
- Nico has built up a pension fund of £600,000, whereas Erin's, funded by part-time work, is £120,000.
- They have savings of £100,000.

In the above scenario, it can be confidently predicted that there is likely to be an equal division of capital and of pensions, and Erin will also have a claim for spousal maintenance for herself from Nico until such time as she can stand on her own two feet, probably when the pensions are in payment. It doesn't matter that Nico is the sole owner of the family home; the Court will exercise its wide powers in favour of Erin to achieve a fair outcome, and to ensure that there is no discrimination based on 'who did what' during the marriage.

Now consider what would happen with identical facts but with the difference that Nico and Erin never married. The startling reality is that:

- Erin would have no automatic claim to any capital resources belonging to Nico (as opposed to belonging to them both), probably not even the family home.
- She would have no claim to share in Nico's pension funds – even though she had prioritized caring for their children at the expense of making her own contributions.
- She would have no claim for maintenance.

Now imagine that Nico and Erin never married but their children are 14 and 12, instead of 10 years older. In that scenario, Erin is able to mount a financial claim for specific capital sums if the children need them, including for housing for a period of time, but only until the children are adults (when any property will revert to Nico, regardless of Erin's needs at that stage). Erin can also obtain child maintenance. But once the children no longer require financial support, her claims on their behalf will end.

If they never married, it doesn't matter that Erin subordinated her own career prospects to the needs of the family, or that by doing so she cleared the decks for Nico's career to flourish. Legally, there is no claim that Erin can bring for her own benefit, for capital, maintenance or a share of pensions. The scale of Nico's wealth makes no difference either – it doesn't matter if he is a millionaire or a pauper. The contrast with their married contemporaries is stark.

Your children, if you have them

'So, what about the kids?'

From a legal perspective, this is much more straightforward. We don't need to be told the basics of our job as parents – to love and care for our children, educate them, keep them safe and meet their emotional and physical needs as they grow and develop. In short, to provide them with a secure and happy home life, as best we can.

'What does the law say about our roles as parents?'

The legal basis of the authority by which parents arrange things for their children – for example, decisions about schooling, medical procedures, or which religion they follow – is something called 'Parental Responsibility'. PR is essentially a description of status, a legal umbrella term for

all the rights, duties, powers, responsibilities and authority which by law a parent of a child has in relation to the child and his property[7]

Most parents hold PR for their children, and in Step 7 we will go through in more detail the circumstances in which you do so. The bottom line is that if you have PR, you must use it to further the welfare of your child. All holders of PR are obliged to work together to achieve this aim.

But you are absolutely not under any obligations to obtain Court Orders setting out what you have agreed, nor to have the Family Court approve the arrangements. The law will happily entrust such decision-making to parents. Indeed, there is a legal principle that the Court will not make *any* orders regarding children unless doing so is better than not doing so (known as the 'no order' principle).

'But what if we aren't going to be able to agree? What can the Court do then?'

As we have already seen, Court intervention should be left only for those cases where there are genuine welfare issues at stake, for example where the current arrangements are causing harm. These are, thankfully, comparatively rare.

If you have exhausted all other options, then as a last resort the Family Court has wide powers to:

- direct a professional enquiry into your family's circumstances, with a view to making recommendations as to how best to promote your children's welfare
- make orders as to with whom children should live and when, and with whom they should spend time
- make orders as to specific issues concerning their welfare, such as which school they should attend
- make orders preventing a parent exercising their PR in a defined way

We'll consider all of this further in Step 7.

Bear in mind that if you apply to Court, you are entrusting a Judge neither you nor your children have ever met before to make critical decisions in relation to your family. As parents, you are surrendering control. Your PR will be overridden.

AMY AND ADRIAN

Amy has PR in relation to TJ as his mother, as does Adrian as an unmarried father who is named on the birth certificate. So, both parents have the same rights and responsibilities in relation to TJ. Each has an obligation to exercise those responsibilities to promote TJ's welfare, as well as to consult each other over any issues that arise and to make plans for the future.

There is a positive duty upon Amy and Adrian to work together. Neither is in a position to dictate to the other.

But they cannot agree on the arrangements for TJ, so ultimately the Court intervenes. It is now up to the Judge to determine the best way forward. Amy and Adrian are left with the task of implementing the Judge's order, whether they like it or not.

OVER TO YOU ...

Is there anything urgent that needs thinking about?

Hopefully you will be beginning to form some clearer ideas of the nuts and bolts of separation and in the broadest terms where you stand from a legal perspective. Here are some common aspects which you may want to start thinking about:

Relationship status
If you are married, do you know yet whether you want to divorce?
- At some point you'll need to decide whether you want to divorce or not, and, if you do and you are an international family, in which country ('jurisdiction') you wish to proceed. Please note that this book relates to the laws in England and Wales. If you have a connection with another country, the rules will be different and you should seek independent legal advice urgently.
- If you already agree you want to divorce in England and Wales, explore whether you would like to apply jointly for a divorce under the new no-fault divorce rules.
- Do you need any external professional support to reach agreement on the above?

Your finances
What about the current living arrangements?
- If you're still living together under the same roof, you'll need to agree what the arrangements should be whilst you work to resolve the wider issues. If one or both of you does not feel safe, then you must urgently take independent legal advice. Do you want legal advice anyway, before you can decide this issue?
- If one of you is going to be moving out, can you agree where to? You'll want to consider:

» The type and quality of housing needed. Will children be living or staying there? Is this just a stop-gap solution or for the longer term?

» Geography. Are you restricted to a particular location for work or childcare?

» There will be rent or mortgage payments, utility bills, council tax, service charges, ground rent, set-up and moving costs.

» What will be the impact on the wider family finances? If you are spending limited resources setting up another home, this may have a significant impact on what is left over for other family expenditure, particularly discretionary expenditure.

» Tax (again), in particular if you have significant resources. The date you separate is important from a Capital Gains Tax (CGT) perspective. Take accountancy advice.

• If money is going to be tight, it might be worth exploring what measures you can agree to take to reduce your outgoings on the family home, at least for a limited period. Some options might include:

» Whether a mortgage 'holiday' can be arranged. Will your lender defer payments for a short period of time?

» If you presently have a repayment element to your mortgage, can it be converted to interest only?

» Are you entitled to Council Tax reduction?[8]

Tax

• Consider whether you need tax and legal advice on the timing of any divorce proceedings.

• You might also need urgent tax advice on the timing of any transfers of assets between you, where already agreed. If you are in the tax year of separation, you should take advice from an accountant about this, as there can be significant tax savings in transferring assets during the tax year in which you separate.

Work, jobs and benefits

• Do you know if your employer has a divorce policy aimed at supporting you? If not, do you know what informal support can be given in terms of

flexible working hours/time off to enable your participation in the
separation process?

- If money is tight, are you presently maximizing your earning capacities,
  taking into account any childcare and other commitments?
- Are you receiving all state benefits to which you are entitled? Find out,
  using gov.uk information on where to find benefits calculators.[9]

Borrowing money

- Do you need to borrow money to make ends meet for now, and if so, where
  from? How do you strike the balance between meeting your present needs
  and not undermining your future prospects? Take financial advice.
- Should you repay money previously lent by family members, if this is
  agreed? Is this affordable at present?
- Should you repay money previously lent by family members, if this is not
  agreed? Consider carefully whether this is likely to create difficulty
  between you and your former partner at this stage, and be aware that any
  unilateral steps you take can, in certain circumstances, be 'undone' by the
  Court adding the money you transferred back into the pot.

Children

We are going to go through these issues quite carefully in the next step, but for now
here's a list to start mulling over.

'What do we tell the kids?'

- Having decided you are separating, if you have children and if they don't
  know already, have you both agreed when and how you are going to tell
  them? Have you agreed what support they will need?
- If you're in new relationships which are likely to endure, have you decided
  when and how you are going to tell the children about them? Have you each
  met each other's new partners? Do you need some help navigating these
  conversations (many parents do)?

Childcare arrangements now that you're living apart

- This isn't the time to make long-term plans. We are going to help you navigate co-parenting choices in Step 5, before looking at the legal landscape in Step 7. For now, we just want you to think about the next two to three months and make a list of the issues you need to agree for the short term:
  » How are you going to manage the day-to-day care of your children, ensuring they spend meaningful time with each of you whilst fitting around your respective work and life commitments?
  » Are there any special occasions coming up, such as birthdays, school events, Mother's Day, Father's Day, Christmas, Easter, Eid, Diwali or Passover? If so, you will need to agree how you are going to manage those in a way which works for your children.
  » Are there any school holidays coming up? Have you agreed what the plans are?

The above doesn't aim to cover every urgent question which may arise – everyone's lives are different. But hopefully you can set the agenda for yours. If you are struggling, reread Step 3 and discuss the support you need. You aren't expected to agree on everything. This will take time and perseverance.

STEP 5

||||||||||||||||||||||||||||||||||||||||||||||||||||||||||||||||||||||||||

STARTING TO TALK ABOUT THE CHILDREN

||||||||||||||||||||||||||||||||||||||||||||||||||||||||||||||||||||||||||

*'What is effective co-parenting and
how do we do it?'*

It's 3 a.m. Your youngest child has a very high fever. Your other two are sleeping, and you are the only adult at home. You are, understandably, panicking. Should you go to hospital? Is that an over-reaction? But then, better safe than sorry, surely? But what do you do with your other two? Wake them and take them with you?

It's a scenario most parents experience at least once, often several times, during their children's early years. No matter how many times you go through it, when you think your child needs emergency medical help, it is extremely stressful.

Focus on this: who do you call? For most parents, the person most receptive to that 3 a.m. call is the other parent. We are all different. We all parent differently. We all show love differently. But a sick child is a leveller for us all.

What we should say now, at the outset, is that if you have escaped an abusive relationship, or are looking to do so, this step is not for you. Your safety and that of your children are paramount.[1] You cannot co-parent in the way we will describe here with an abuser.

So, let's assume there is no abuse dynamic, but that you and your former partner just aren't getting on. Maybe you've only recently separated, and emotions are still very raw. Perhaps one of you has a new partner, which is creating tension. The division of your finances may be driving a further wedge between you and causing angst. So you think twice about calling. You run through the list of other people you can call. Not because your co-parent won't drop everything to be there, but because it's, well, just too *awkward*.

ESTABLISHING CO-PARENTING

Think about what you're giving up if you don't co-parent

When people talk about co-parenting after divorce, understandably most of the emphasis (sometimes the only emphasis) is on how much better it is for the child. Yup. Understood. But we want to talk here about what co-parenting means for *you*. Or rather, what you're giving up if you give up on co-parenting.

Parenting is hard. It is relentless, monotonous, unpaid and, at times, will drive you to the limits of your patience. Yes, it's also magical, but let's be realistic. It's hard.

There is a respectable school of thought that says that the reason we humans have survived to dominate the planet for so long is our unparalleled ability to care for one another – for partners, children, families, friends, fellow humans. We are hard-wired to bond.[2] Not that we are all hard-wired to be perfect parents, or co-parents. Far from it. You may now, as you read this, be listing the many ways in which your former partner is far from the perfect parent. Maybe you're also being harsh on yourself. Don't be. For now, we don't want you to think about your current situation, but to think about this in the abstract. Wouldn't it be great to know you could always call your co-parent in an emergency, even at 3 a.m.? Wouldn't it be brilliant to go on a weekend away knowing your children could happily spend time with their other parent and there would be no resentment?

Don't idealize the past, focus on the future

Divorce, like many life changes, involves giving up some things and gaining others. Here's how parents getting divorced might see it:

- 'I'm losing half my time with my child.'
- 'I'm going to be less of a parent.'
- 'I'm not going to tuck them into bed each night, or help them with their homework every day.'
- 'This is going to make us less close.'

Here's how we'd like you to start thinking about it:

- 'This divorce is giving me the chance to *improve* my relationship with our child.'
- 'No more weekends filled with tension or sniping, because our marriage wasn't working.'
- 'Time without our child is going to be a big adjustment, but it will give me an opportunity to recharge and look after myself in a way I never could before.'
- 'We can make new traditions now, and choose the way we spend our time together.'
- 'This could make me a better parent, and make us *closer*.'

Don't idealize the way things were before. And don't catastrophize the future. Frame of mind really matters. If you start anticipating the worst, you'll deprive yourself of so many wonderful opportunities, because you'll be too blinkered to see them.

Perhaps this is best illustrated by another case study.

JAN AND MICK

Jan and Mick have been living together for 12 years. They have never wanted to get married.

They have one child, Lucy, who is six years old. She was a longed-for rainbow baby, after many years of unsuccessful IVF and miscarriages.

Jan has a senior position at an investment bank. Mick works long hours as an orthopaedic surgeon. He recently secured a consultancy post, which Jan was hoping would give him more control over his hours, but it doesn't seem that this has happened yet. Jan's earnings are far higher than Mick's, which wasn't an issue in the past but now creates tension when childcare emergencies arise and Mick's work affords him little flexibility to help.

The end of their relationship wasn't explosive or sudden, but a slow burn of disappointment and growing resentment. This was no longer a relationship which could meet either of their needs and was, in different ways, making them both extremely miserable.

Mick has been offered the opportunity to borrow the flat of a friend who has secured a six-month secondment to Hong Kong. It seems a good way to give him and Jan some space as they figure out their next steps. He says yes instinctively, without checking with her first.

When he tells her, she feels blindsided, and rejected all over again. Suddenly the talk of separation has turned from something abstract into reality. She doesn't know if this is what she wants. Certainly, she wanted more say in when and how it happened. She feels ambushed.

Mick is very surprised by Jan's emotional reaction. She was the one who first suggested separation. He is exhausted by what he sees as her unpredictability. He thinks space will do them both good, so he goes ahead with the move.

And within this vortex of emotion is Lucy. She still needs all her physical and emotional needs met, just as she did before. The school run has to happen each morning. Play dates have to be navigated, aversion to vegetables tolerated and manipulated, bedtime stories read.

There are a myriad of ways this could play out. Let's take two, at the extreme ends of the spectrum.

Scenario One

Jan cannot get past the fact of Mick leaving. She replays it endlessly in her mind. Him packing. The way he didn't look back when he got in the car. For her, this is no longer a separation. She has been abandoned. Left to her own thoughts, she forgets that she was the one who originally suggested separation, that the relationship had been failing her, that they were both unhappy. Instead, she clings to Lucy. In her mind, the situation morphs from 'Jan being left' to 'Jan and Lucy being left'. Mick has left her to parent alone and she becomes increasingly sceptical about Lucy spending time with him. Lucy wants to be at home, not in that pokey flat. Mick was never around anyway. He's hopeless at the school routine, always forgetting the right kit. He can't even do Lucy's hair properly. What Lucy needs right now is stability and consistency, and that's her home. Mick can see her during the day each weekend, perhaps for a Saturday afternoon outing. It feels too soon for her to stay overnight at the flat. She won't settle. But Mick keeps asking for more.

Mick thought moving out would make things better. But now Jan won't even look at him and their text messages are curt. He stops trying to improve things with her. They're separating anyway; what's the point? Clearly they weren't right for each other. His focus shifts to Lucy. Moving out impacted him more than he anticipated. He desperately misses being able to go into her bedroom late at night and hear her breathing whilst she sleeps. He misses rearranging her covers. Whereas during the relationship he was happy for Jan and the nanny to cover all the parenting logistics during the week, now he feels he has to make more time for Lucy so he doesn't lose the relationship. He speaks to his work and manages to secure two days a week when he can leave in time to collect Lucy from school. Jan has been asking him for years to 'step up', so he thinks she'll be pleased. When she says she doesn't think Lucy spending that much time with him is right at the moment, he panics. His emails to Jan become more forthright: when will overnights start? He proposes schedules for the progression of Lucy's time with him. Jan, he feels, is fudging her responses and committing to nothing.

In the middle of all of this is Lucy. She knows her father has moved out. She has seen her mother crying. Above all, she senses the tension when they are together. She starts to dread the times when she has to see them together – the handovers.

Lucy is distressed when moving between her parents' homes. Jan feels this shows she doesn't want to spend as much time with Mick, even though he is pushing for more and more. Mick sees Lucy's upset when her mother is there, but once they drive away she's fine. So what is going on? He starts searching on the internet and reads about parents who don't see their children at all because the other parent has 'poisoned' the children against them. Is that what is happening here?

Mick decides enough is enough and he starts legal proceedings. We'll continue this story in Step 7.

Scenario Two

Jan is devastated about Mick leaving. Their texts are curt and things aren't good. They both recognize this and decide to meet at a coffee shop. They don't try to agree on anything, or to make plans for the future, they just acknowledge that things are bad. And that if they're going to co-parent Lucy the way they want, things need to be better.

They go and see a co-parenting expert. They each have an individual meeting first. Jan talks about her feelings of abandonment. Mick opens up about his fear of losing Lucy, of being less of a father now. He explains that this separation is shining a harsh light on the practical side of parenting that he hasn't taken the lead on before. He feels inept – at worst, superfluous.

In their joint sessions together, Jan and Mick slowly share these feelings and fears and are given concrete ways to overcome them. They are both able to acknowledge that they want Lucy to have a good relationship with each of them. That they still want to be a family. Mick invites Jan to visit the flat and she and Lucy help to decorate the spare bedroom to make it more Lucy-friendly. Jan carefully plans her time the first weekend Lucy is away, organizing things she wouldn't be able to do if Lucy were with her – some yoga, dinner with friends, daytime Netflix! Mick recognizes and appreciates the effort it has taken Jan to manage the nanny, the endless school communications and the changes of kit.

Jan and Mick are still the same people. They still have the same flaws. They will still fall out, sometimes about petty things, sometimes about major things. They will still criticize each other's parenting. But they have strategies to work through those bumps. They have a plan.

Above all, they are learning how to be happy parents apart. So Lucy can be happy.

||||||||||||||||||||||||||||||||||||||||||||||||||||||||||||||||||||||||||||||||||||||||||||||||||||||||||||||||||||||||||||||||||||||||||||||||||||||||||||

What did Jan and Mick do differently in the second scenario? They communicated. They recognized they needed help and they got it. They didn't remain in their own silos of fear and resentment, projecting the worst possible version of the other person onto them. They remembered their co-parent was a fellow human being, not a caricature. And they built the skills they needed, not to put Lucy first, but to put their family first. By caring for themselves and caring for each other, they were caring for Lucy too.

WHAT DO THE EXPERTS SAY?

This feels like a good time to call in the experts. And no, in this scenario, that's not us! As you have no doubt picked up by now, we believe lawyers are great for legal advice, but when it comes to co-parenting, and adapting your adult relationship to fit that new mould, you need much more than just legal advice. Which is why, when we developed our own co-parenting service at The Divorce Surgery, we felt it vital that parents shared not only a lawyer but also a co-parenting expert, to give them the practical skills and strategies to master the art of successful co-parenting post-divorce.

The co-parenting expert we brought in was Bill Hewlett. Bill is a post-separation family repair specialist. He is a mediator and a child consultant, and he helps separating parents to come to cooperative and collaborative agreements about their children. We'd worked with him for years in private practice, often sending him cases that seemed destined for a long and messy trial, only for him to talk the couples back from the brink. So you can get the benefit of Bill's expertise first-hand, Samantha recorded a chat with him for this book.

By the way, if you're anxious about the lack of law in this step, fear not! We cover it in Step 7. But for now we're working on soft skills which, believe it or not, are likely to get you better long-term results than any legal solution.

Samantha: It's so lovely to be able to include you in our book! To kick off our conversation, I really want to ask you what your definition of a good divorce would be?

Bill: It's interesting that divorce is perceived as something that's not a good thing. In many ways, it's just something that happens to people – a lot of people. And, you know, a divorce can be a time of enthusiastic optimism about what's possible in the future. For people who have struggled and been unhappy with each other for a really long time, it can be a great opportunity to finally get their relationship into a state where they actually get on quite well.

Samantha: I love this aspect of what you're saying, and I totally agree with it, that a divorce or separation is an evolution. And can be the start of something better and different.

Bill: Yes, it's a time for the family to reshape itself. It's an opportunity for everybody finally to live a life that is more in accordance with what they always wanted. People get together in a relationship and it seems fine and they work out certain ways of being with each other over time. But when the relationship stops working so well and they don't feel so great about each other, that is a great opportunity to reinvent the family in a new form. It's actually a time for optimism and positivity.

Samantha: And in practical terms, how does a couple approach divorce with a positive mindset?

Bill: Therapists often talk about how an interaction between two people is very much driven by how it begins – what they call a soft and harsh start-up. I think we can relate that concept to how people manage divorce. If they start well, it will probably end well. So if you come to divorce with the idea that, hey, things have changed, we need to rejig our family, then what could possibly go wrong? We've got two people, both parents who want their kids to be OK and the situation between the two of them to be better. Why wouldn't it be?

Samantha: You make it sound so simple! What do you think is holding us back as a society from this positive messaging?

Bill: I definitely think there needs to be a lot more education. As a society, we pay insufficient attention to the fact that if things get difficult between Mum and Dad, if it gets hostile and angry, there really are some serious long-term consequences for children. It's also really important to understand what happens to people who are in relationships that don't work out. If you understand that your feelings of personal hurt, loneliness or shame are not unusual, are feelings that many others share, then you won't feel that something is wrong with you. This is just how it feels. So I think a deeper, broader, wider understanding and appreciation of what happens when people get to this point in their lives needs to be known and understood.

Samantha: Yes, absolutely. I wish every divorcing couple knew about the 2019 research by the Family Justice Observatory, which found that high-conflict Family Court proceedings can cause emotional harm to the adults and children involved. And it called it out as a public health issue. I am sure no divorcing couple ever anticipates where Court proceedings might lead in terms of impact on their mental health, or that of their children. We both work with families across the spectrum: from very early stage, those who may be just considering separation, to those who've been in entrenched litigation for some time and are just desperate to find a way out. I wonder, from your experience, what you think it is that drives couples to Court and what can be done to stop it?

Bill: We don't reflect enough on what drives couples to Court. People want vindication. They want some person in authority to say they've been really badly treated and that they're a good person. But that's a relationship issue, not a legal one. The Courts don't have the time, the mechanisms or the necessary knowledge to assist people with what are essentially relationship problems. What couples need is not a Court process but one which involves them each at some point acknowledging the other's experience. That will never happen in an adversarial process.

Samantha: I think that is just such a good point, because I see it so often in Court proceedings. I know that really what one of the parties wants is some recognition by the other. It might just be a thanks. It may be an acknowledgement of the sacrifices that have been made over the years. But communication has completely broken down, so they're not even speaking. And that recognition isn't something that lawyers can get for them. It isn't something a Judge will give. Judges don't pronounce winners and losers, they're just looking for a pragmatic solution for a family. In fact, they generally bend over backwards to ensure no one feels that they've 'won', because they know how damaging that can be for their children. So it's an incredibly ineffective tool if what you want is some kind of recognition or acknowledgement.

What's disappointing is that we have so few examples in real life of couples who have navigated divorce together and well. And it's really hard to emulate something if you can't see somebody who has done it and talked about it. If we had more examples of what it feels like – that it will be hard at times, but that it's so much better in the long run – then more couples would have the confidence to see it through.

Bill: In the UK, going to separate lawyers is the standard first step. And of course the lens you look through determines what you see. We start people off in a tough, adversarial process which makes them angry. So it's no wonder we don't see many great examples of how to separate, because what's on offer, generally speaking, is a process which pitches you against each other, making you angrier and less able to work together.

Samantha: Absolutely! You need to start in the right mindset or it becomes a self-fulfilling prophecy. If you start thinking it's going to be contentious and awful, then it's going to be contentious and awful, because the first time you hit a bump in the road, you'll think, 'Here I am in this awful process, just as I imagined.' Whereas if you believe it's going to be OK, despite the bumps in the road, then you'll come out with that mentality too.

Bill: How you begin, as we were saying before, determines where you end up. Co-parents need a clear understanding that if they want the kids to be OK, they need to look after each other. And I know that's the last thing people want to do. But if kids experience their parents undermining each other, if kids experience their parents feeling bad about each other, then they're going to have to deal with that. They're going to have to repair it. If Dad's made Mum feel really bad, the kids are going to have to help Mum feel better. And if Mum has done something to Dad that made him really sad, the kids are going to have to step in and cheer Dad up. So the key is helping parents understand that the best way to look after their children is to look after each other. And I know that kind of goes against every part of what they're feeling, because the relationship is broken down. They're angry, they're hurt, they're upset. It feels very counter-intuitive. But they need to be mindful of the fact that the children's very well-being, their welfare, their capacity to thrive as people, very much depends on Mum and Dad being able to bring out the best in each other, even though this is a really tough time.

Samantha: I also try and get people to think about the adult loss in not having a cooperative parenting relationship. If you're in a situation where you have no support from your co-parent, you're putting so much onto yourself in terms of burden, and that builds resentment in itself. I always talk about the feverish child at 3 a.m. – who do you call?

Bill: That's really true. Thinking about that 3 a.m. call, if you had a sense that the other parent would say, 'Thank you for ringing, I really feel appreciative that you've included me, how can I help?', then of course you'd call them. So it's good to help both parents understand what sort of response you need to get if you ring up at 3 o'clock in the morning. How would you like that person to behave towards you? How would you like to feel? How would you like to think they think of you as a parent? That can be sorted in no time at all.

Samantha: So, getting to the nub, why is it so important for separating couples to address their relationship as co-parents rather than just think of divorce as a legal issue?

Bill: When life doesn't go well for us, we become very narrow in terms of our thinking. We generally hold someone else responsible or blame them. We lose perspective. Getting into conflict is often what humans do when life doesn't work out. It's an old, deeply established reaction that goes back to when we were living in a much more dangerous world than we are now. And refusing to countenance that we might not be 100 per cent right is a natural human reaction to things not going well.

If there aren't any kids in the mix, well, I guess that's a way to recover, although it's not ideal. But when one person has to be right, that means the other person has to be wrong, and if there are children in the mix, that's a very dangerous way to recover from something not working out, because then they are caught in the middle. So be reflective, allow yourself to have some insights into your part in what has happened and how others might have felt, rather than just dropping into a very simple blame narrative that says the answer to every question lies in the bad character of the other person. Seek a broader perspective.

Samantha: I'm a big fan of having a shared big picture, because I think you're then much, much less likely to fall out over the details. When people have been in litigation for a while, everything becomes so granular. The high-stakes fight over six nights a fortnight or seven has come about because there isn't a shared vision of what the future is going to be like. And that means fear takes over, which is often the fear of being less of a parent than they were before. But if parents have a shared vision about what their new relationship is going to be like and what their children's experience is going to be, then they're much less likely to resort to arguments about specifics, because they have trust. So they can be flexible. And that's the hope, isn't it, that we can create a scenario where co-parents don't need strait-jacket Court Orders to be able to communicate and agree arrangements which are bound to flex over time.

Bill: Yes. You can't legislate a relationship. What we do as a species when we're upset is we always try to describe our upset through events and behaviours that occurred. So, when we say, 'You were late picking me up,' we're actually trying to communicate something much deeper: 'I feel hurt, I feel let down, I feel abandoned. I feel that you don't care about me.' But we frame those comments in language that is about an event, a thing that happened. And of course, the other person doesn't like being criticized or told that they're not a good person. And so they react by saying, 'No, I didn't do that thing on that day. You're wrong.' So the emotion we're trying to communicate to the other person, which is 'I feel hurt', gets lost in the detail.

Then if the Courts get all caught up in the details, we're all missing the point. That people feel hurt and actually doing something about feeling hurt is quite easily attended to if we can find some way to acknowledge a person's hurt. It's actually so simple, and yet people go through these long, arduous, complicated, expensive, aggressive adversarial processes. And all that is needed is for the other person to say, 'You're right. You were hurt. I am sorry.'

We just need to help separating couples cut to the chase: to acknowledge each other's experiences and be heard. Getting to that quickly will save them from a long, awful, drawn-out Court process that won't give them any sense of acknowledgement, but will focus solely on conflict, which is really the sideshow.

Samantha: So those early conversations are crucial, aren't they? About the relationship and what the legacy of that relationship will be. And what each person wants for the future. Because then they can start thinking logically about big decisions and legal advice. But if the emotion is ruling everything else, then it's hopeless, actually.

Bill: It's so crucial to have a conversation where the couple acknowledges that the problem is not so much their characters, but more the way their relationship managed their differences. Everybody has differences, everybody has different ideas about parenting, education and health. We all have strong core belief systems that we hold dear. When we speak about those things that really matter to us and the other person doesn't agree, we can feel very hurt. We feel personally attacked when they say, 'I don't believe in private schooling,' or 'I don't think our children should be vegetarian,' because that person has attacked something that is very core to us. As co-parents, you need to find a way to discuss those core issues without being in conflict. And to understand that it's your relationship (and not the other parent) that let you both down in the past.

Most people go into relationships in good faith. They try as hard as they can. But the relationship may not have enabled them to see the effort the other person has been making. For some reason, it set them up to fail. That's the relationship's fault, not the couple's fault.

Sometimes I quite like the analogy of two people going to a car yard and buying a car together. Looks like a great car. It's all shiny. They take a long, long drive and it turns out the car is a lemon. It just doesn't work. They spend the rest of their lives blaming each other for the fact that they bought the car. But they bought it in good faith.

So it's important to identify what needs to take responsibility, and that's the *relationship* rather than the couple.

WHAT ABOUT THE CHILDREN?

We've focused here on the adults and their relationship. Because, genuinely, for the vast majority of families, that is the key. Your children will take their lead from you. But if you need any further incentive to work together for the sake of your children, here are some extra motivators.

The Family Justice Young People's Board is an extraordinary group of over 50 children and young people aged between 7 and 25 years old who live across England and Wales. All have either direct experience of the Family Justice system or an interest in children's rights and the Family Courts. They work closely with stakeholders within the Family Justice system to make it child-centred and child-inclusive. We have had the privilege of hearing some of their members speak about their experience of Family Justice. It was distressing and humbling, and underlined, more than ever, the way a child's voice can be utterly lost in contested Court proceedings.

These children created 25 top tips for parents to help them think about matters from their child's perspective.[3] It's a powerful list:

1. Remember I have the right to see both of my parents as long as it is safe for me.
2. I can have a relationship with the partner of my other parent without this changing my love for you.
3. Try to have good communication with my other parent, because it will help me. Speak to them nicely.
4. Keep my other parent updated about my needs and what is happening for me. I might need their help too.
5. Don't say bad things about my other parent, especially if I can hear. Remember I can often overhear your conversations or see your social media comments.
6. Remember it is OK for me to love and have a relationship with my other parent.
7. Don't make me feel guilty about spending time with my other parent.
8. Don't make permanent decisions about my life based on how you feel at the moment. Think about how I feel now and how I might feel in the future. My wishes might change.
9. Be open to change, be flexible and compromise when agreeing arrangements for me.
10. It's OK with me if my parents don't do things exactly the same. You are both different, and that's alright with me.

11. Don't be possessive over me and the things that belong to me. Make it easy for me to take the things I need, such as school work, PE kits, clothes, books, games, phone, etc., when I spend time with my other parent. Let me choose what I want to take with me.

12. Keep me informed about any changes to my arrangements.

13. Try not to feel hurt if I choose to spend time with my friends instead of seeing you. I am growing up!

14. Remember that important dates (birthdays, celebrations, parents' evening, sports day, etc.) are special to you, me and my other parent. I may want to share my time on those dates with each of you.

15. Work out between you and my other parent who is responsible for the extra things I need, such as new school shoes and uniform, school trips, dinner money and the cost of my hobbies or after-school activities. I don't want to be involved in this.

16. Remember that I don't expect you or my other parent to be perfect, so I don't want you to expect my other parent to be perfect either. Accept mistakes and move on.

17. Make sure I am not left out of key family events. Please compromise with my other parent so I can join in.

18. Please don't stop me having contact with extended family members who are important to me. Ask me how I feel about them. Don't assume my feelings are the same as yours.

19. Don't use me as a messenger between you and my other parent.

20. Don't use my relationship with my other parent against me, or them.

21. Don't ask me to lie to my other parent or other family members.

22. Don't ask me to lie to professionals, or to say what you want me to say.

23. Don't make me scared to say what I think about my arrangements for fear of being told off or treated badly by you if you don't agree.

24. Remember that I might want something different to my brother or sister.

25. Don't worry about how others see you or what they think. I am what matters.

No doubt you have read that list and feel fortified that Court proceedings are the last place you want to be. As you'll know from Step 2, Family Judges agree with you. But be aware of the statistics. Around 125,000 households with dependent children in England and Wales separate per year. Of those, evidence suggests that a third end up using the Family Courts.[4] Which is a huge proportion of the separating population. And shows the extent to which going to Court has become normalized. But it shouldn't be normal. Again, research has shown that the Court process *itself* risks escalating conflict to a point where it becomes harmful to children. So remain fortified, and take that through to the next exercise.

OVER TO YOU …

Starting to talk about your children

Right, now is the time to dip your toes in the water and to explore how you want your co-parenting relationship to be.

There are two big questions, and we want you to make a list of the answers. Ideally we would like you to do this together, although you can draw up your own lists and then exchange them, if that works better for you as a starting-point.

1. 'What do we want our reshaped family to be like?'

Go big-picture Hollywood-movie aspirational in your answers here! Remember this is a once-in-a-lifetime opportunity to make things better. You will be co-parents for the rest of your lives. How you manage this transition will impact those lives, not to mention those of your children.

Here are some ideas:

- 'I want to be able to call you at 3 a.m. without hesitation, and without feeling judged.'

- 'I want our children to call us a family. I want us to feel like a family.'
- 'I want us to respect each other as parents.'
- 'I want us each to recognize each other's strengths, and the effort we each put in to parenting.'
- 'I don't want us to criticize each other.'
- 'I want us to work past our issues with each other away from our children, so we can nail being parents.'
- 'I want our children to grow up with a good relationship with both of us.'
- 'I don't want to push you out. I don't want to do this alone.'
- 'I want us to be the first person we talk to about our children. We will form new adult relationships, and I want us to find a way to navigate those.'

On this last point, bear in mind these words from divorce and family dynamics coach Nichole Farrow: 'Three out of four people go on to remarry, and having an amicable divorce and a healthy relationship with your ex pays dividends in your relationships and your children's relationships in the future.'[5]

2. What is on the agenda?

Now isn't the time to reach agreements about specifics. But it's good to have a broad understanding of where you're heading, and where the sticking points might be. That way you can contextualize the difficulties and swerve around some of the bumps in the road. If you have very different parenting styles, or if one of you has more hands-on experience of the school routine, that may be feeding into more granular anxieties about how the children should move between your homes. If you are getting support from a co-parenting expert or divorce coach, even just for one joint session, it's good to set out clearly what it is you anticipate being hardest to navigate.

For that reason, at the end of this step we've included a parenting plan. It's adapted from one produced by Cafcass, the Children and Family Court Advisory and Support Service (*see Resources*).

Please know that you really don't need to have a parenting plan. If you're working well together, you may find it annoyingly prescriptive. In that case, please don't start filling it in! And if some of the questions cause tension between you, shut the book. The last thing we want is for it to uncover issues you hadn't even identified. All we want you to do at this point is glance through the plan and give yourselves the opportunity to spot the issues you're pretty sure you'll agree on and those which may need to go on the agenda. That's it.

|||||||||||||||||||||||||||||||||||||||||||||||||||||||||||||||||||||||||||||||||||||||||||||||||||||||||||||||||||||||||||||||||||||||||||||||||||||||||||||||||||||||||||||||||||

Perhaps at this stage you'll seek some professional support with your relationship. Perhaps you'll take some time to reflect. Let it all percolate for a while. We won't be looking at the law relating to children yet.

The next step, when you're ready, is back to the finances. That's Step 6. When the time is right for you, let's get started.

A PARENTING PLAN

(An amended version of the parenting plan produced by Cafcass, the Children and Family Court Advisory and Support Service[6])

We respect each other as parents and our significance in the lives of our children.

We have drawn up this parenting plan to assist us in providing a loving, stable, caring and safe environment for our children, in line with their age and needs.

We recognize our children's rights to:

- emotional and physical safety, stability and security
- feel loved by both of us and significant family members
- know and be cared for by both of us and significant family members, and
- develop independent and meaningful relationships with each of us

As parents, we accept responsibility for:

- our children's physical care, health and safety
- our children's emotional stability
- our children's changing needs as they grow and mature
- protecting our children so they are not exposed to harmful parental conflict that is prolonged or aggressive
- cooperating with each other to make decisions in our children's best interests; and
- respecting our children's relationship with each of us

Safety

We have considered our safety and welfare and that of the children and agree that we can work together safely.

Questions about communication

- What parenting decisions do we need to consult each other about?
- What parenting decisions don't we need to consult each other about?
- How are we going to behave towards each other in front of the children? We want them to know we are getting along and have them in mind.
- How are we going to share important information with each other (for example, school reports, health issues)?
- Do we need regular meetings to discuss parenting issues?
- How do we find out what the children want to happen, and make sure that they have a say in what we decide?
- At what times is it OK to call the other parent and when isn't it OK?
- How will we settle disputes?
- Should we discuss how we talk to the children about the other parent?
- How will we talk to the children about the arrangements we have made?
- What do we do about emergencies (for example, medical, dental or accidents)?
- How will we make sure our children stay in contact with supportive friends or relatives from the other side of the family?
- How will we introduce new partners to our children's lives?
- Are there any important rules that we consider essential for the children (for example, bedtimes, when homework is done, staying out late)? Do we agree that these rules are to be followed?
- How do we work together to make the big decisions (for example, school, course selection and careers advice)?

Questions about living and childcare arrangements

- Will there be a main place where the children will live, and if so, where will it be?
- If neither of us can look after the children, who will be the alternative carers? What about school holidays?

- Are there times when it is not convenient to ring our children?
- What sort of communication will we have with the children (phone, text, email) and when and how often can they expect it?
- How much time can each child spend with each parent?
- What days can they be with each of us?
- How do we make sure that the children can share special days – birthdays and religious festivals – with both of us?
- How can we maintain close and meaningful contact if we and the children are separated for long periods of time?
- How will we manage the arrangement if one parent works long hours?
- What clothes and other belongings will be taken and returned at changeover?
- How will we arrange pick-ups and drop-offs?
- Who will take the children to regular sporting engagements at weekends? After school?
- When and how will we make sure the children are seeing their grandparents?
- Will anyone else look after the children (for example, childminders, babysitters, relatives, new partners, friends and neighbours)? If so, when?
- What are the arrangements for the children during the school holidays? (Consider bank holidays and teacher training days as well as school holidays.)
- How do we make sure that we both have holidays with the children and plan for taking the children abroad (if we agree they can go)?

Questions about education
- How will we deal with the school and get them to send notices, reports and other material related to our children's progress to both of us?
- How can we get involved separately, as parents, in the school?
- How should we make contact with school counsellors so that they know about our separation and how it might affect the children?

Questions about health and other issues
- Who organizes routine health issues?
- Are there long-term health issues that we need to consider?
- What do we agree about religious practice and upbringing?

- Are there any other cultural issues that we need to make sure are respected?
- Are there any sporting or artistic commitments that we need to account for?
- Are arrangements needed for the family pets?

STEP 6

||||||||||||||||||||||||||||||||||||||||||||||||||||||||||||||||||||||||||||

BUILDING OUR FINANCIAL PICTURE

||||||||||||||||||||||||||||||||||||||||||||||||||||||||||||||||||||||||||||

'How do we go through our finances?'

Before you continue reading, know this: for many, many people we advise, finances are simply not their thing. They find the prospect of trying to find answers to the questions we set out here at best daunting, and at worst terrifying. If you feel the same way, please don't panic! Know that such feelings are completely normal. And it's why most couples will need professional support with their finances.

To put it another way, we all have different strengths within our relationships. We might be a ninja with an investment portfolio, but struggle profoundly with the emotional side of divorce. Like anything in life, you recruit for your weaknesses. So if finances scare you, take this opportunity to get some help. As we discussed in Step 3, many financial advisers are now specializing in divorce, so you can find help in working through your own finances, and be educated as you go, so you feel confident at the end that you truly understand and can take control of your money.

Here we'll look at financial disclosure, which is in essence the process by which the Family Court works out what there is in the pot to divide. Dividing it fairly is the task we undertake together in Step 8. So if you would like to jump to Step 8 first and then come back to this one, that's completely fine. Go for it. You'll then have an understanding of where you're going to end up, before coming back to the detail of financial disclosure.

OK, let's get started. Financial disclosure sounds (and may actually be) boring, but it's the cornerstone of any fair financial settlement. It's dry, but fundamentally necessary.

Why? In every case where you are seeking to divide your resources *fairly*, the first question the Court will ask is: 'What is there to divide?' The logic is that you cannot sensibly carve up the cake without first knowing how big it is.

This basic principle applies to whichever route you end up choosing to resolve your financial issues, whether it be joint legal advice using One Couple One Lawyer, mediation, two-solicitor negotiation, arbitration, going to Court, or something else. Whatever you choose, you just can't do the job properly without financial disclosure.

Be aware that at this stage in the process you are probably going to need some legal advice and, depending on the complexity of your finances, some financial advice and very possibly some tax advice too. As ever, try to access such advice jointly. Embarking on financial disclosure doesn't have to be confrontational in any way. And if you work together, transparently, you can build up a financial picture in which you can both have confidence.

THE DUTY OF FULL AND FRANK DISCLOSURE

In divorce proceedings, you are each under a duty to provide full, frank and clear disclosure (known as the 'duty of full and frank disclosure') both to each other and to the Court. What are we talking about exactly? Essentially, disclosure is the business of setting out the building blocks of your financial life: your assets; your pensions; your income. And of course, on the other side of the ledger and just as important, your liabilities.

The task at hand is to identify these resources and liabilities and to put a value on them.

The identification part is usually comparatively straightforward: most people tend to know *what* they've got, or at least where to start looking. The valuing part is often much harder, but that really depends on the nature of the asset you've identified – it might be easy enough to discover what's in your bank account, but valuing a shareholding in a private company can be very difficult, and in some cases not realistically possible. We'll come back to valuation issues later on.

Crucially, the duty of full and frank disclosure is not confined to providing details of what you have right now, or at the point of settling. The concept also extends to the financial rights and obligations that you'll have in the future, where already known. One obvious example would be if you were to settle your financial arrangements on the basis of your current earnings and decline to mention that you were on the cusp of taking a much better-paid job elsewhere. This would be a clear breach of your duty.

It is worth emphasizing that the duty to disclose applies to each of you, irrespective of who ran the finances during the relationship. Granted, it might be a much more onerous task for one of you. But it is not enough simply to rely on your former partner to discharge your duty for you.

What are your responsibilities if you are *not* in Court proceedings, don't intend to be and are simply seeking to resolve things consensually? The precise answer will depend on the rules of engagement of the scheme you have chosen, but whichever voluntary process you choose will make it a condition of your participation that you both agree to give full and frank disclosure. So in practice this means there is little or no difference to the information to be provided, whether you are inside or outside a Court setting.

We'll get into the question of *how* you give full and frank disclosure later on.

When is financial disclosure not required?

The most common reason *not* to require or give disclosure is if it would not be *proportionate* to do so, or that the information in question is simply *irrelevant*. At its most basic, ask yourself whether the disclosure being requested makes any difference to the issues at hand. Then ask yourself how hard and/or expensive it would be to get the disclosure.

These days, provided you can remember your online log-in details, it is really very easy, cheap and quick to get hold of most categories of disclosure – bank statements, insurance policy documents, share certificates, premium bonds and so on. But if one of you had, say, a foreign bank account many years ago for a brief period prior to your marriage, but no longer has any details of the relevant bank or your account, and you are very sure it doesn't contain anything interesting, then a Court wouldn't expect you to move Heaven and Earth in the name of completism. There is a cost/benefit analysis to be done.

Legal advice plays a vital role here: without it, it can be hard to know what the issues in a case actually are, and therefore what disclosure is relevant/proportionate and what is not. That in turn will depend on your personal circumstances – how long you were married, whether you have children, the standard of living during the marriage and so on. It all depends.

Be aware that you cannot be made to disclose to each other confidential advice given to you by your independently instructed lawyers, if you have them. That is basically sacrosanct, other than in some very limited circumstances. If you are seeking joint advice, then of course you are both privy to the same legal advice, and your shared lawyer will give you both an objective view as to what disclosure is proportionate in your particular situation. This enables the exercise to remain transparent.

'But what if I am prepared to agree whatever figures my former partner puts forward?'

Be very careful. If you have no means of verifying important aspects of your financial landscape – a valuation of a pension fund into which you know your former spouse has contributed for the last decade, for example – then you are opening yourself up to significant risk. Ask yourself why this information is not being made readily available. What efforts have been made to get it?

It is understandable that former partners working together to separate amicably will want to cut each other some slack, but this must have limits. If you are the one resisting disclosure, then again, ask yourself why. Are you building in obstacles to working together by refusing to provide something which is reasonably requested?

Also be aware that for some assets the face value may not represent its true value. This is particularly the case for pensions, where the cash equivalent value (the number given on your pension statement) can be far less than the real value of the benefits you will receive in retirement. This point was emphasized in the Pensions Advisory Group report,[1] which recommends pension valuation by a Pensions on Divorce Expert (PODE) in all cases where there are pension assets over £100,000, or other complicating factors such as public service pension schemes.

Bear in mind that if you agree not to require disclosure of an asset your shared lawyer or separate lawyers have identified as relevant, their legal advice will probably be caveated to that extent.

And remember, the duty to disclose is owed to the *Court* as well, not just to each other.

'What happens if there is inadequate financial disclosure?'

Then we're back to the problem we identified at the beginning of this step: if you don't know what there is, how can you begin to divide it fairly? For divorcing couples wanting their finances resolved by binding Court Order, will a Judge approve your deal?

What's more, if you do settle but one of you later discovers there has been non-disclosure, there is a risk the Court may set aside its order.

SHARLAND AND SHARLAND [2015]

Mr and Mrs Sharland married in 1993 but separated in 2010, having had three children. Mr Sharland owned a substantial shareholding in a software business, which became the matter in dispute between them.

Expert evidence of the valuation of the shareholding was obtained, and Mr Sharland gave evidence that there were no plans for an Initial Public Offering (IPO) of shares in the company 'on the cards today'.

The case settled by agreement during the trial, with Mrs Sharland to have 30 per cent of the sale proceeds of the shareholding whenever that might happen. But before the Court Order was finalized, Mrs Sharland became aware that the business was being readied for an IPO, which would have valued the company far in excess of the assumptions used in the negotiations.

It became clear that Mr Sharland had known about a possible IPO all along, but had dishonestly omitted to say so. The Judge, however, concluded that had he known about the fraud, he would have made the same order anyway.

After extensive, and no doubt expensive, legal argument in the High Court, Court of Appeal and finally in the Supreme Court, the case was reopened and sent back to the High Court to be redetermined.

||||||||||||||||||||||||||||||||||||||||||||||||||||||||||||||||||||||||||||||||||||||||||||||||||||||||||||||||||||||||||||||||||||||||||||||||

That is obviously an extreme example. But the underlying principles apply just as much in cases where the assets are less substantial.

As well as the escalation in legal fees, stress and uncertainty caused by going back to square one, non-disclosure will affect your confidence in each other and your prospects for a cooperative relationship in the future. Non-disclosure cases are amongst the most emotionally fraught encountered by lawyers specializing in this area.

'So, how do we give financial disclosure and what is a Form E?'

If as a divorcing couple you were to proceed through the Court system, you would each be required to produce a document called a Form E.[2]

Filling it in can be a somewhat daunting process, first because it's 28 pages long, and secondly because it says this at the front:

> You have a duty to the Court to give a full, frank and clear disclosure of all your financial and other relevant circumstances. A failure to give full and accurate disclosure may result in any order the Court makes being set aside. If you are found to have been deliberately untruthful, criminal proceedings may be brought against you for fraud under the Fraud Act 1996. The information given in this form must be confirmed by a statement of truth. *Proceedings for contempt of Court may be brought against a person who makes, or causes to be made, a false statement in a document verified by a statement of truth.*

In other words, you have to declare that what you are disclosing is true, and if it isn't, there may be serious consequences.

In terms of ramming home the message that financial disclosure has to be accurate, full and clear, the Form E has much to recommend it. So for that reason, many out-of-Court processes use this too. Another benefit is that if, despite your best endeavours, you end up in the Family Court, you won't have to start from scratch when compiling your documents.

Fortunately, help has arrived when it comes to filling out the form itself. Rather than the tiresome business of doing so by hand, or manually inputting figures into a Word or pdf document, lawyers have recently begun to develop much more client-focused technologies to make this easier. At The Divorce Surgery, we use specially designed software to ask clients a series of questions about their finances in clear, easy-to-understand language specifically designed to address the requirements of Form E. The answers given then automatically populate the form for couples to review, approve and, when ready, sign. What's more, you are only asked the questions that apply to your specific situation, so you aren't obliged to wade through pages of queries relating to family trusts or pre-nuptial agreements if those aren't relevant to you.

But in summary, you have to disclose any interests you have in:

Capital
- land and buildings, together with details of any mortgages
- bank, building society or savings accounts
- investments, including in shares and premium bonds
- life insurance policies
- any money that is owed to you
- any cash you hold in excess of £500
- any belongings worth more than £500
- any liabilities you have, including credit cards, loans, hire purchase agreements and tax owed

- business assets (whether as a sole trader, a partner in a partnership or a shareholder in a limited company)
- pension funds
- any other resources to which you may be entitled, for example Trust assets, or assets held on your behalf by a third party

Income
- any earnings from employment
- any earnings from self-employment or partnership
- any income from investments (such as dividends, interest or rental income)
- any income from state benefits
- any pension income

Note that all of these obligations extend to your *worldwide* resources, not just those held/received in England and Wales. What's more, you have to give details of any significant changes in assets or income in the last 12 months, as well as any you think are likely to occur in the next 12 months. If you are in a new cohabiting relationship or have remarried or formed a civil partnership, you will also have to give details of your new partner's resources, so far as you know them.

The Form E also asks you to give details of the more subjective aspects of your financial life together, including:

- the standard of living enjoyed during the marriage
- any particular contributions either of you have made, or anticipate making, to the family finances or to family life which you think should be taken into account
- any other relevant circumstances, including inheritance prospects, disability, retirement plans, remarriage plans and so on
- any 'bad behaviour or conduct' by your former partner, if you feel it should be taken into account. Spoiler alert: It practically never is, though we'll say more about this in Step 8. For couples who are committed to working together, 'conduct', as it's known, can be safely ignored.

Be aware that the Form E also requires you to provide a considerable quantity of documentation in support of your figures, including, for example: 12 months of bank statements for every account you operate (whether dormant or not), dividend counterfoils relating to any shareholdings (however insignificant), and so on. But if you're in an out-of-Court process, you have more flexibility to dispense with the irrelevant and focus on the things which really matter.

Don't help yourself ...

Tempting as it is, you must resist the lure of helping yourself to your former partner's financial information. This used to happen all the time, until the Courts stamped all over the practice in a case called *Tchenguiz and Others v Imerman* [2010].

The very clear position today is that it is unlawful to access confidential information belonging to another person, even if you are married to that person, whether by email or other online means, or, more traditionally, simply going through their post or paperwork. Depending on how you access the confidential information, you may also be committing criminal offences. If you find yourself in that position, you should take independent legal advice without delay.

Of course, if you're already working together effectively, none of this will apply to you. But even if you are not (yet) doing so, taking matters into your own hands in this way is likely to raise the temperature and make settlement harder than ever.

MARK AND DAVID

You may recall this couple from Step 3. They had very different ideas about what a fair financial settlement might look like. In the end they took legal advice and reached an agreement, but let's go back in time for a moment and look at the early days of their financial discussions, before they had any professional support.

David recalls seeing some documentation at the family home which he thinks will demonstrate his key point – that Mark's business did really well during the course of their marriage together. Because relations with Mark have deteriorated, he does not fully trust him to disclose those documents in due course.

Worried that he won't be able to obtain them any other way, David decides to help himself. One day, he takes some internal company documents from the closed drawer of Mark's desk whilst he is out of the house, marked 'Management Accounts – confidential'. David copies them on his phone and returns the originals to Mark's desk.

The documents show that, contrary to the impression Mark has now been giving, the business' growth accelerated during the marriage. David feels relieved that he has some proof.

David's position is understandable, but not justifiable from a legal perspective. Mark and the company both have clear expectations of privacy in relation to the material David has taken. David is potentially exposing himself to Court proceedings, including for damages, as a result of his unlawful taking of Mark and the company's documents. The consequences for David might be very serious indeed.

What David should have done was await Mark's obligation to provide the material, as part of Mark's own duty of full and frank disclosure. If Mark did not provide satisfactory documentation at that time, he would be in breach of his duty.

David will now have to delete any digital or other copies of the material he has taken.

Clearly Mark and David are not yet working together constructively. But David has raised tensions considerably by unlawfully accessing Mark's confidential information. Mark's position that David is only 'in it for the money' has hardened. David now feels on the back foot.

VALUATIONS

Of course, not all assets have a straightforward, unarguable 'value' like cash does, or the value of some Royal Mail shares at a particular moment which (being a public company) you can simply look up online. Houses and flats, for example. How much is a house actually *worth*? Various online property websites might give you an idea, as might your research about comparable sales in your road, but in the end a property is only worth what someone ends up paying for it.

So when it comes to giving disclosure of these types of assets, the task is more complicated. There is usually not just one answer, but a range of *opinion*.

When there is disagreement over the value of an asset, the Family Court tends to get around this problem by permitting you jointly to instruct someone with the relevant expertise to provide a valuation which you can then both rely on. Normally, the Court accepts that valuation for the purposes of establishing what your resources are. Of course, you won't want to obtain – or pay for – valuations unless they are really necessary in order to progress your settlement discussions. However, sometimes they are unavoidable. You'll often need early legal advice to help you decide.

Here are some common types of asset which might need valuing:

The family home, or other investment property

'Who does a valuation?'

Estate agents, or for more complex situations and properties, a chartered surveyor.

'When do you need one?'

If you cannot agree the value of your home or other property assets, you'll need some way of finding a figure to use for your negotiations. For most, the family home is likely to be the most valuable asset a couple owns, so it can make a huge difference to your discussions if the valuation is £50,000 more or less than one of you thinks. A common exception to this is when you agree that you are going to sell and have decided on the marketing price – in that case, you will know the value of the property when it sells.

'What will it cost?'

Most estate agents will do a market appraisal for free. If you need a more in-depth valuation, particularly if the property in question has unresolved structural or planning issues, an estate agent or surveyor will invariably give you a fixed-fee quote beforehand.

'What else do I need to know?'

If your property assets are not very substantial and/or complicated, most couples tend to resolve valuation issues by obtaining market appraisals from three or more local estate agents who know the area. They then take the average of the three and agree to use that figure as the value for settlement discussions.

Company assets

'Who does a valuation?'

You'll need an accountant who has experience of valuing company assets in divorce. Family lawyers work hand in hand with accountants all the time and will be able to give you some recommendations.

'A valuation of what, exactly?'

Of any *shareholding* you have in a *private limited company*, and often also an assessment of whether any value can be extracted from the company whilst it continues to trade ('liquidity') and of any income the business can produce moving forward. By contrast, the value of shares in quoted *public* companies (e.g. Apple, or BP) is freely available online and in newspapers, and in general does not generate valuation issues.

Take legal advice

You are very likely to need legal input before you charge off to instruct a valuer. It may be completely unnecessary to spend scarce resources valuing your interest in a company; alternatively, it might be unavoidable. Take advice as to the proportionality of obtaining a valuation in your specific circumstances, and of what needs valuing and how.

'What will it cost?'

Valuing a company is unlikely to cost much less than £4,000 + VAT and may be many multiples of that, depending on the complexity of the issues. You will want to agree fixed fees before you start.

'How long will it take?'

Again, this will depend heavily on the complexity of the issues, as well as the availability of the information the valuer needs to provide the report.

Tax liabilities

'What help do I need?'

If you have one, your accountant will be able to tell you whether you owe any unpaid income tax (relevant for the self-employed and those with income from investments) or Capital Gains Tax, and what it amounts to. If you don't have an accountant, do some research to find someone suitably qualified who can help you in relation to this issue.

They do not need to have specific experience in advising separating couples, but it helps. Don't forget any overseas tax liabilities you may have.

'What will it cost?'

This will depend on the complexity of your finances, but if all you are after is some basic CGT calculations, you are unlikely to be charged for more than an hour's work.

'How long will it take?'

Obviously individual practices will vary, but if your accounts are in good order (i.e. the accountant does not have to piece together your finances over past years), then most will turn around some basic calculations in two to three weeks. It's worth noting that if you want CGT advice relating to the tax arising on disposal of second homes/properties, you will need to have agreed figures for *those* valuations first, before you approach the accountant.

Pensions

'Pensions seem really difficult ... Can't we just forget about them?'

Absolutely not, if you're a divorcing couple. Research by Manchester University in 2021[3] found that pension wealth is very unequally distributed between separating individuals:

- Men have far more in private pensions than women, with rising inequality across age groups. For those aged 65–69, median pension wealth for men is just over £212,000 compared to just £35,000 for women.
- Fewer than 15 per cent of couples have pensions that are approximately equal. For about half of couples with pensions, one partner has 90 per cent of the pension wealth. These disparities are broadly consistent across the income and wealth distributions.

- For households in the top 40 per cent by household income, median pension wealth *exceeds* median property wealth.

This latter point chimes with a 2019 report by the Pensions Advisory Group (the PAG report),[4] which made the point that after the family home, pensions are often the next largest family asset and that 'Ignoring the pensions or agreeing to ignore the pensions is not an option.'

In short, there is a growing awareness that women are losing out very substantially in pension terms. The Family Court will want and expect to see that pensions have been appropriately dealt with before approving any consent order.

'*What help do we need?*'

As a first step, divorcing couples will need valuations of each pension fund either of them owns (usually referred to as the 'Cash Equivalent Value'). Each pension fund will send you an updated valuation statement regularly. But, depending on the type of pensions you each have, the headline figure provided may not represent the true value of the benefits that pension will pay out on retirement. Nor will it tell you anything about how pensions can be divided between you, or what the impact of transferring a proportion of your fund to your former partner would be in income terms for either of you. For that, you will need a report from a Pensions on Divorce Expert.

'*What are we asking the Pensions on Divorce Expert to do?*'

Again, it depends what the legal issues in your case are likely to be, so you may wish to take legal advice first. Broadly, though, the expert will be looking at how to divide pension assets between you so as to meet each of your needs in retirement, based on the factual scenarios you identify. So if, as an example only, you want the expert to look at how to achieve equality of income for you both from the pensions you have each acquired during the marriage, then the expert will identify how those pensions would be split to achieve that and what the equalized income in retirement would be. Your lawyers will guide you.

'What will it cost?'

Unlikely to be much less than £1,000 + VAT, and maybe as much as £3,000 + VAT or more, depending on the number of pension funds and the extent of the issues being considered. Pensions on divorce is a very specialist area, so it is important to use an expert who has relevant experience. Appendix D of the PAG report contains a certification which any expert you instruct should sign, confirming they have the appropriate expertise.

'How long will it take?'

It is not at all unusual for pension reports to take six to eight weeks, and often longer. A major source of delay is awaiting up-to-date pension fund valuations from the pension fund trustees, which can take many weeks.

These are just some examples, but of course you can get more or less anything valued if you really want to – cars, art, furniture, antiques, jewellery and so on. Bear in mind at all times proportionality, however. Is a valuation really necessary, or is there a figure you can both live with to enable your discussions to proceed? You'll want to concentrate your budget where it is really needed.

'How do I go about instructing an expert?'

You will need a joint 'letter of instruction' setting out what it is you are asking the expert to do, timescales and of course, the agreed cost. It's important to be specific about what you want (particularly when it comes to business valuations) – if you aren't, unnecessary costs can build up quickly. If you have one shared lawyer, they will be able to draft the letter of instruction for you both, covering the areas that are relevant. If you have separate lawyers, ensure the drafting of the letter of instruction does not become a disproportionately costly exercise.

There are (thankfully rare) cases where it takes weeks or sometimes months to agree the letter of instruction. Keep perspective and ensure you aren't spending legal fees unnecessarily.

'We've completed our Forms E and given them to each other ... What if I have concerns about my former partner's disclosure?'

It depends ... Most of us are somewhere on a scale of ignorance about our partner's financial affairs (and often even about our own). Sometimes that ignorance is near total: many people remain more or less entirely dependent on a partner to administer their joint financial affairs during the course of the relationship. In such cases, it is normal, if not inevitable, that you will feel vulnerable and anxious about money issues upon separation. Often what helps is sitting down together with a financial adviser to talk through your finances, so you both understand what there is and any tax consequences, and then taking legal advice, together or apart, as to what further disclosure or expert valuation is needed (if any). We find one of the most reassuring aspects for the divorcing couples we see is the knowledge that an experienced family law barrister, instructed by them both, is going to review all their financial disclosure impartially and highlight if anything needs further clarification. This means that couples can do their best, safe in the knowledge that it is going to be carefully reviewed.

Try to distinguish between general feelings of anxiety about money on the one hand and specific disclosure queries on the other. And even if you do have specific disclosure queries, don't rush to judgement. Not every failure to provide disclosure is a sign of dishonesty. Maybe one of you hasn't appreciated the relevance of a document, or considers producing it is disproportionate to the wider issues.

Fundamentally, though, if you don't have confidence in the information your former partner is providing and/or if you think they may be hiding assets, then you must seek *urgent independent legal advice*.

NEEDS: ASSEMBLING THE EVIDENCE

Building your financial picture is partly about looking back at what you've accumulated over the course of your relationship and partly also about looking forward to what comes next. What do think you each *need* to move forward independently?

We'll consider how the law deals with 'needs' in much more detail in Step 8, but as a starting-point the Court will want some information from each of you about how you see things panning out.

We'll look at needs from both a capital and income perspective. They are usually heavily interlinked.

Capital

The major capital need all of us have is for suitable housing. Where are you each (and, if you have them, your children) going to be living? What sort of housing is going to be required? What will it cost?

If you think buying another home is realistic for one or both of you, can you get a mortgage, and if so, how much can you borrow and what will it cost each month? To answer those questions you are probably going to need two things:

1. An illustration of your mortgage capacity

For a small fee, a mortgage broker will be happy to set out your mortgage capacity based on your earnings. Some lenders are also prepared to take into account maintenance payments, particularly when paid as part of a Court Order. They'll also need to know what your regular outgoings are (*more on this below*). It's sometimes helpful to get an illustration of what the monthly repayments would be both on a repayment and interest-only basis, if that flexibility is needed. There is no reason you can't use the same mortgage broker to look at each of your circumstances, for consistency of approach.

Alternatively, a more rough and ready indication can be had from an online mortgage calculator. Again, use the same one if you can.

Then, take financial advice, also together, as to what you can actually afford. Be realistic and avoid wishful thinking: the consequences of a decision to borrow too much will reverberate for many years, particularly when an initially attractive fixed rate expires. What happens if and when interest rates eventually rise?

2. Estate agents' property particulars

Factoring in your mortgage capacity, look online to see what's suitable and available in the area you have identified for housing. Again, you aren't trying to identify the *actual* property in which one or other of you will be living, more what is out there in your price bracket.

If you aren't the one moving out, ask yourself whether you could imagine yourself in the type of property you have identified. Is this somewhere you can see your children being happy? Is the location workable, bearing in mind work commitments and/or the school run?

There is no getting away from the fact that, for most couples, the standard of living enjoyed when they were together will not be available to them once separated. Two households are more expensive than one. You have to expect that and be prepared for it.

Does undertaking this exercise make you reflect on whether it is feasible to retain the family home?

If you're hoping to buy, don't forget tax and moving costs. You can work out the tax you will have to pay on purchasing a property via the HMRC Stamp Duty Land Tax calculator on the gov.uk website.[5] On top of that, you'll have conveyancing costs to pay, as well as removal costs, survey fees and local authority search fees.

Income

A different but related point concerns your budget. What are you going to live on each month?

Go through your bank statements for the last 12 months to work out what you actually spend. But, as we've seen, just because you've been used to spending at a certain rate in the past is no guarantee that you'll be able to do so in the future. After a separation, it is painful, but usual, to make economies. If rent, for example, now has to be afforded on top of your usual outgoings, that is going to blow a big hole in your previous spending assumptions.

For most people, housing costs, whether mortgage or rent, will be the major expense, together with utilities and council tax, so working those out first is usually sensible.

Here is a basic budget to get you started. Obviously not every line will apply to you.

SCHEDULE OF OUTGOINGS		
TYPE OF EXPENDITURE	£ per month	£ per annum
Household expenses:		
Mortgage		
Mortgage protection premium		
Life assurance policy premium		
Insurance – buildings		
Insurance – contents		
Burglar alarm		
Rent		
Ground charges		
Service charges		
Council tax		
Water rates		

Electricity		
Gas		
Oil		
Telephone		
Mobile telephone		
TV licence		
Subscription TV		
Cleaner		
Gardener		
Window cleaner		
Repairs and maintenance		
Redecoration		
Sub-total:	**£0.00**	**£0.00**
Housekeeping expenses:		
Food and groceries		
Wines and spirits		
Newspapers		
Magazines		
Stationery		
Chemist		
Household cleaning materials		
Garden		
Sub-total:	**£0.00**	**£0.00**

Personal expenses:		
Clothes		
Shoes		
Accessories		
Dry cleaning		
Shoe repairs		
Hairdressing		
Cosmetics		
Toiletries		
Beautician		
Dentist		
Optician		
Contact lenses		
Prescriptions		
Gifts		
Charity donations		
Pets		
Cinema/theatre, etc		
Eating out and takeaways		
Club subscriptions		
Health club/gym		
Flowers		
Sports (and equipment)		

Holidays		
Hobbies		
Christmas expenses		
Sub-total:	**£0.00**	**£0.00**
Car and transport expenses:		
Insurance		
Servicing/MOT/maintenance		
Road tax		
Fuel		
Parking costs		
Roadside assistance membership		
Depreciation		
HP agreement		
Public transport costs		
Car wash/valet		
Sub-total:	**£0.00**	**£0.00**
Other personal expenditure:		
Pension contributions		
Maintenance to former spouse or children		
Medical/permanent health insurance		
Medical bills/prescriptions		
Other – please specify		
Sub-total:	**£0.00**	**£0.00**

Children's expenses		
Clothes		
Shoes		
Haircuts		
Nappies		
Nursery fees		
Babysitting		
Nanny		
Presents		
Eating out		
Health club		
Magazine subscriptions		
Toys		
Pocket money		
Holidays		
Public transport costs		
Mobile telephone		
Sub-total:	**£0.00**	**£0.00**
School expenses:		
Travel to school		
School meals		
School fees		
School outings		

School extras		
School uniform		
School footwear		
Sports clothing and footwear		
Sports equipment		
Music lessons/tuition		
Music lessons/instruments		
Riding lessons		
Dance/ballet lessons		
Swimming lessons		
Tennis lessons		
Driving lessons		
Sub-total:	£0.00	£0.00
TOTAL:	£0.00	£0.00

If you find this difficult, there are a number of excellent (and inexpensive) accountancy services specializing in helping with budget preparation and cash-flow modelling, as we discussed in Step 3.

Unmarried couples

As you'll be aware by now, the law treats married and unmarried couples very differently at present.

If you have children together

If this is you, then, as we saw in Step 4, your rights to bring financial claims against the other party are restricted to those that can be justified as being for the benefit of your children.

Of course, your financial disclosure must still be full, frank and clear. But as a starting-point, the obligation on each of you to provide financial information is not quite as broad or deep as it is for your married counterparts.

Why? Essentially because the Court's job is different. Here, the Court is not trying to divide the totality of your resources in a way which is fair, but is instead aiming to meet your children's needs, which is not the same thing at all. In short, there is often less that it will be relevant or proportionate to disclose. Reflecting this, in Court proceedings, unmarried parties are not required to complete Form E (although they sometimes agree to do so anyway), but a shorter version called a Form E1.[6] This document carries all the same warnings as to the need for truthfulness, but asks for less in terms of narrative.

If you don't have children together

If this is you, then, as we have already seen in Step 4, you have no financial family law-based claims against each other, and no consequential disclosure obligations. If you own property together, or at least one of you considers that you do, then you can ask the Court to determine your shares, and as part of that litigation, orders for disclosure will be made, relevant to the issues in that case. This is a specialist area upon which you should take advice from a lawyer specializing in such civil property claims.

||||||||||||||||||||||||||||||||||||||||||||||||||||||||||||||||||||||||||||||||||||||||||||||||||||||||||||||||||||||||||||||||||||||||

OVER TO YOU ...

||||||||||||||||||||||||||||||||||||||||||||||||||||||||||||||||||||||||||||||||||||||||||||||||||||||||||||||||||||||||||||||||||||||||

'So, how do we put all this into practice?'

Assembling your financial disclosure will take time and patience. Preparation is key, as is doing things in the right order. Having the information at your fingertips before you start will save you a lot of time in the long run.

You'll need to set aside sufficient time to do this, so it's important to be realistic. As a rule of thumb, unless your finances are particularly straightforward, to 'do' financial disclosure well using a Form E will probably take at least four weeks, and that's before obtaining any valuation evidence.

Here is a suggested timetable, for when you both agree you're ready:

Week 1

- Identify where and how you're going to get legal advice. Jointly or independently?
- Download and read a Form E. Do not start filling it in yet.
- Begin to assemble the financial information you'll need. Focus on the aspects that are likely to be time-consuming to obtain. In particular:
    » Do you have your pension statements to hand, or do you need to request them from your pension fund?
    » Can you agree any property valuations? How far apart are you at the moment? If you're not far apart, can you agree to split the difference so you have an agreed figure for your discussions?
    » Identify any other significant assets which you think may need valuing.

Weeks 2–3

- Take legal advice. What valuation evidence do you think you might need, if any? If you decide to proceed, what is it likely to cost and what issues will it address? How long will it take?
- Begin work on identifying your capital and income needs for the future:

- » Approach a mortgage broker or use an online mortgage calculator to identify your mortgage capacities.
- » Conduct online research to identify potential housing solutions and share details of any suitable properties with each other.
- » Fill out the income needs schedule. Get help if you need it.
- Begin filling out your Forms E.

Weeks 4–5

- Finish filling out both Forms E. Take legal advice as you go if you need it.
- Exchange the Forms E when you are both ready.

Week 6 onwards

- Review each other's Form E. Are you satisfied with the information provided, or do you have questions? If you do, ask them.
- Take legal advice, either together or separately, to ensure (a) that the disclosure is complete and (b) whether any expert input is required for valuation purposes.
- If expert input is needed, this is the time to get your lawyer to draft a letter of instruction, jointly select an expert and get them going. When the expert report comes back, you may have more questions. Ask those too.

Obviously, if you need longer, that's fine. It's much more important to get your disclosure right than to do it quickly. And of course, life intervenes. Perhaps you have to focus on your children for a few weeks, or your job, or your own well-being. That's all fine too.

When you're ready, if you wish you can leapfrog to Step 8, which is where we set out the law that forms the backdrop for reaching a fair financial agreement. If you have children, though, you should first stop by Step 7, where we look at reaching a co-parenting agreement.

REACHING A CO-PARENTING AGREEMENT

'What if we can't agree what is right for our children?'

The very first and most important thing to know is that it isn't always obvious what the right arrangements for your children should be. And if one solution is obvious to one of you, a completely different scenario may seem intuitively right to the other. When you're dealing with children, the goalposts are constantly shifting. What is best for them will inevitably change as they get older, and in the meantime there are likely to be regular variations depending on what's going on: illnesses, crucial work meetings, endless school events. Life, as we know, has a habit of getting in the way of even the best-laid plans.

So please start this step knowing it is completely normal *not* to agree with your fellow co-parent. In fact, your differing perspectives will be *helpful* if you look at them in the right way. If you work from the (extremely likely) starting-point that you both want what is best for your children, you can use your respective suggestions as a way of setting the agenda (rather than red lines to hide behind). As we discussed in Step 5, if you can get to the nub of where your proposals are coming from (for example, a fear of being marginalized as a parent/wanting to be more hands on/anxiety about how your child will adapt), then you are much more likely to reach a consensus.

In our experience, although many of these issues are *not* best resolved through a purely legal lens, it can really help co-parents to have a high-level understanding of what the law says (and, importantly, where a Judge will be unable to help them) as they navigate these important conversations.

So as part of Step 7 we aim to give you both just that: a high-level understanding of how the Courts approach decisions relating to the arrangements for children on divorce. It isn't a textbook. Nor is it legal advice, as this will inevitably vary for each and every one of you, depending on your particular family circumstances. But it should hopefully empower you both either to reach your own co-parenting agreement or to focus on the areas where you may need some tailored legal advice, which you can then access either impartially and together or from separate lawyers.

Health warning

This will not apply to you or your children if you are in a relationship which puts you at risk of emotional or physical harm. Your safety, and that of your children, is paramount. Seek urgent, independent legal advice and know that the Courts have emergency powers which they can and will use to protect you where needed.

'WHO DO WE MEAN WHEN WE SAY "PARENTS"?'

Families come in all shapes and sizes. Diversity is a wonderful thing, and no two families are the same. Courts have recognized different types of natural parenthood, including genetic parenthood (provision of gametes), gestational motherhood (conceiving and bearing of children) and social and psychological parenthood (the relationship that develops through the child demanding and the parent providing for the child's needs).[1]

When we refer to 'parents' in this step, it's a shorthand for anyone who holds parental responsibility (PR) for a child.

Parental responsibility

As a reminder, parental responsibility is a legal relationship between an adult and a child and encapsulates all the decision-making power and authority needed to provide effective long-term care for that child. Parental responsibility holders can make decisions, for example about the child's home, care, education, religion, discipline, medical treatment, emigration and adoption. Having parental responsibility for a child does not entitle a person to act incompatibly with a Court Order, however, and there are some important restrictions, for example changing a child's name or removing a child from the country without the other parent's consent.[2] As stated by Lord Justice Ryder in Re D [2014]:

The concept of parental responsibility describes an adult's responsibility to secure the welfare of their child, which is to be exercised for the benefit of the child not the adult.

You will automatically hold parental responsibility if you are:

- The birth mother (although this is the legal drafting, happily families now are regularly formed with the assistance of surrogacy, adoption and other arrangements. This is a specialist area outside the scope of this book, but if you are concerned about your legal status as a parent, do know that there are a number of family lawyers who are specialist in this field and will be able to help.)
- The child's father or second female parent if the parents were married or in a civil partnership at the time of the child's birth.
- In circumstances where the child's father is not married or in a civil partnership with the mother, he will acquire parental responsibility if he is named on the child's birth certificate.
- In circumstances where the second female parent is not married or in a civil partnership with the mother, she will acquire parental responsibility if the treatment took place in a clinic licensed by the Human Fertilisation and Embryology Authority and relevant consents were signed prior to treatment.

There are other situations in which you may automatically hold parental responsibility, for instance if there is a Court Order providing that the child lives with you.

Even if you don't automatically hold parental responsibility, for instance if you are a step-parent, you can acquire it by agreement with the other parent (and you would then enter into a 'parental responsibility agreement'). If you would like to have parental responsibility but this is not agreed, you can apply to the Court for such an order to be made, and the Court will assess your degree of commitment to the child, the child's attachment to you, the reasons why you are applying for the order and all other circumstances, with the child's welfare as the paramount consideration.

'If I've read this, do I still need legal advice?'

Not necessarily. And in that respect, this is very different from Step 8 (concerning the division of your finances).

Family Courts start from the basis that the best people to make decisions about children's care are their parents (and those who hold parental responsibility). This underpins the 'no order principle', at section 1(5) of the Children Act 1989, which, as you will see, is the key legislation when the Family Courts are dealing with children:

> Where a court is considering whether or not to make one or more orders under this Act with respect to a child, it shall not make the order or any of the orders unless it considers that doing so would be better for the child than making no order at all.

So, if you both agree the arrangements for your children, the Court will not interfere. There is no supervisory element, as there is when it comes to your finances, to ensure your agreement is legally fair. There is no requirement for you to set out your agreement in writing at all (unless that would be helpful for you both, which it often can be). Unless you fundamentally disagree and ask a Judge to become involved in your family life, they won't do so.

But, as we've already discussed, it's normal not to agree. It would be quite strange if there were no areas upon which you had different views about what would work best for your children. You are different people, with different life experiences. You each bring a richness to your children's lives which the other cannot replicate.

This step will give you a high-level view of how Judges make decisions about children and what the Court experience is like. It will help you set the agenda. And that may identify areas on which you would both benefit from legal advice tailored to your circumstances. Importantly, this isn't about delegating the decisions relating to your children, but ensuring you are informed enough to make those decisions yourselves wherever possible.

As we've already discussed, there is a whole variety of professionals who can help you reach an agreement, many of whom are not lawyers, such as co-parenting experts or mediators. But if you decide, as many couples do, that you want, as a backdrop to those discussions, an understanding of the legal position as it applies to your family, then choose your lawyer wisely and set a budget. When it comes to arrangements for your children, be particularly careful not to allow channels of communication to break down. If you can, consider joint legal advice. Don't fall into the trap of convincing yourself that what is best for you is best for your child. It might not be. The perspective of your co-parent matters. An obvious point, but one that often gets lost in the mêlée of contested litigation, is: the only way reach an agreement is to agree. So that means finding a solution you can both accept is right for your child.

'So, what is the law actually trying to do?'

At the heart of every decision a Court makes about a child is one overriding priority: *the welfare principle*, set out at the very start of the Children Act 1989, at section 1(1):

> When a Court determines any question with respect to –
>   (a) the upbringing of a child; or
>   (b) the administration of a child's property or the application of any income
> arising from it,
>   the child's welfare shall be the Court's paramount consideration.

So any decision made by the Family Court has to be in the child's best interests above all else. In any judgment, a Family Judge or Magistrates have to explain *how* the decision made is in the child's best interests. That is the overriding issue driving the Court's agenda. What is best for you, including your right to family life, is not the determining factor.

Three other key principles to bear in mind at this stage are:

Delay is to be avoided

Section 1(2) Children Act:

> In any proceedings in which any question with respect to the upbringing of a child arises, the court shall have regard to the general principle that any delay in determining the question is likely to prejudice his or her welfare.

Of course the kicker here is that Court proceedings themselves cause a significant amount of delay, as you will see when we go through the process of litigation later on in this step. The takeaway point is this: prolonged periods during which you are in conflict are harmful to your children (and to you). This chimes with what we discussed in Step 5 – the emotional harm that can be caused to children by the conflict inherent within Court proceedings. But delay outside the Court process may not necessarily be harmful. So, if you and your former partner are taking your time to decide what is right for your children and working together to achieve that common aim, that is absolutely fine. Delay is only a problem for your children (and for you) when you are all entrenched in conflict and uncertainty.

The involvement of both parents is presumed to be in a child's interests

Section 1(2A) Children Act:

> A court ... is ... to presume, unless the contrary is shown, that involvement of [each] parent in the life of the child concerned will further the child's welfare ... unless there is some evidence to suggest that involvement of that parent in the child's life would put the child at risk of suffering harm whatever the form of the involvement.

It is important to be aware that there is no presumption that children should spend *equal* time with each parent following their separation; 'involvement' just means 'involvement of some kind'. There will be situations where such involvement is not in a child's best interests, in particular where one parent is abusive, but thankfully these cases are the exception and not the norm. The presumption of parental involvement is currently under review by the Government following a 2020 report by the Ministry of Justice which found systematic issues within the Family Justice system affecting how the risk to both children and adults was identified and managed in cases where allegations of abuse were made.[3]

The 'overriding objective'

Part 1 of the Family Procedure Rules 2010:

1. These rules are a new procedural code with the overriding objective of enabling the court to deal with cases justly, having regard to any welfare issues involved.
2. Dealing with a case justly includes, so far as is practicable –
   a. ensuring that it is dealt with expeditiously and fairly;
   b. dealing with the case in ways which are proportionate to the nature, importance and complexity of the issues;
   c. ensuring that the parties are on an equal footing;
   d. saving expense; and
   e. allotting to it an appropriate share of the court's resources, while taking into account the need to allot resources to other cases.

The Family Court is a public resource funded by the taxpayer. Judges must give effect to the overriding objective when exercising any of their powers. Lawyers and litigants are required to help the Court further the overriding objective. What this means is that a Judge will not simply make themselves available to decide any dispute between you. Your case will be given the amount of time a Judge thinks it merits, whether you think it deserves more consideration or not. Increasingly, Judges are urging families to resolve their differences out of Court, and some will adjourn cases to require you to make efforts to settle through alternative means, such as mediation.

OK, with that overview of the key principles which override all decisions relating to children, it's worth exploring what the Courts can (and can't) do.

What are the Court's powers?

A really important place to start is identifying what the Courts have the power to do (and, crucially, what they don't).

Section 8 of the Children Act sets out the orders the Court can make:

> a) Orders detailing with whom and when a child is to live, spend time or otherwise have contact with any person ('a child arrangements order');

What this looks like, in a Court Order, is essentially an instruction requiring you to ensure your child spends set time with, or lives with, each parent. Depending on the extent of your disagreement, this can be as granular as dictating where handovers take place (for example, a car park at a particular service station or coffee shop) and carving up special occasions such as Christmas Day and birthdays. We have included an example order at the end of this step to give you a feel. There is then no room for manoeuvre unless you both agree, so failing to deliver your child to the co-parent at the set time and day is a breach of a Court Order which can result in Court proceedings for enforcement. Perhaps unsurprisingly, research has shown that of those parents who end up in Court, 30 per cent return for more litigation because they end up wanting to change the order and cannot agree.[4]

b) Orders prohibiting the taking of certain steps by a parent who might
otherwise wish to do so in the exercise of parental responsibility ('a
prohibited steps order');

This is a power to stop an exercise of parental responsibility where justified, so, for example, an order forbidding one of you from taking your child abroad or enrolling them in a particular school. But beware: there are many, many parenting disagreements which won't be covered. So you can't turn up at Court and expect a publicly funded judiciary to decide issues such as what types of food you each feed your children, what they wear, what activities they do when they are with each of you, whether one of you buys a pet for your child or how you communicate with each other. Unless any of these choices engage genuine welfare issues, a Judge may simply refuse to deal with them, on the basis that they just reflect differing 'parenting styles'.

c) Orders giving directions for the purpose of determining a specific
question arising in connection with any aspect of parental responsibility for
a child ('a specific issue order').

This is in many ways the converse of the prohibited steps order, so instead of preventing you from exercising an aspect of parental responsibility, this will determine an aspect of that parental responsibility for you, so for instance that your child shall attend a particular school or have significant medical treatment. Again, many of the decisions you each make on a daily basis for your child, including routine medical treatment, will not be issues the Court would consider proportionate to rule on here.

But when will a Judge decide to make an order, and what justification do they need to give for the choices they make? Let's look now both at the laws set down by Parliament and how those laws have been interpreted by Judges in reported cases.

How does the Court exercise its powers?

A key point to know is that Judges operate in a discretionary system. Every family and every child is different. There is no prescribed answer. Almost inevitably you will never get exactly the same decision from two different Judges on the same day. Judges, like all of us, are human beings, and their decisions will be informed by their own life experiences.

The welfare checklist

But in order to ensure a consistent *approach*, the Children Act sets out a list of factors, called the welfare checklist, to which each Judge must have regard when making orders relating to children:

> *(a) the ascertainable wishes and feelings of the child concerned (considered in the light of his age and understanding);*

A child's views are always relevant where they can be ascertained, but the extent to which they influence the overall outcome will depend on a variety of factors, including the child's age, level of maturity and the extent to which their views are considered to be their own rather than influenced by another parent. The way Judges find out what children think is normally by asking a Cafcass Officer (usually a former social worker whose role is to report to the Court) to meet with the child either at home, at school or in the Cafcass office, and explore, in an age-appropriate way, the child's wishes and feelings. This is then set out in a written report which is sent to the Court and shared with the parents. Cafcass resources are very stretched, and increasingly Judges will explore whether such a report is necessary or whether the issues between the parents can be resolved without a Cafcass report being carried out. In very serious cases, a child may need to be represented in the Court proceedings, with their own independently appointed Guardian and solicitor to advocate what is in their best interests.

(b) his physical, emotional and educational needs;

The Cafcass Child Impact Assessment Framework (CIAF) defines emotional needs as 'the needs of a child to feel loved and cared for. Parents and carers should be aware of these needs and communicate with their child in a way that will support the child's positive growth and development'.[5]

(c) the likely effect on him of any change in his circumstances;

This does not mean there is a strict presumption in favour of the status quo. When parents start living in separate homes, this inevitably involves change for children. Some parents try to run arguments in Court that a child's homework routine should not be interrupted by spending time with the other parent. These arguments often carry very little weight with Judges, who will view the need for a child to spend time with both parents as being much more important to their overall well-being than a rigid adherence to the routine imposed by one parent. Really what you should be considering is how to *manage* the inevitable change in the most child-centred way.

(d) his age, sex, background and any characteristics of his which the court considers relevant;

The older a child is, the more the court will acknowledge their ability to 'vote with their feet'. Although judges retain jurisdiction to make orders in relation to children until they are 16 (and in exceptional circumstances, beyond that), in reality judges can be resistant to making orders which teenagers may simply reject. But beware, if you have a teenager, of delegating the decision-making to them, or simply disengaging from the issue of whether they should see their other parent. We have sadly seen cases where children are not given emotional permission by one parent to forge a relationship with the other. This can result in deeply troubled young people, who sometimes, in adult life, reject the parent they lived with in childhood as they forge a new relationship with the other parent.

(e) any harm which he has suffered or is at risk of suffering;

As already highlighted, if you believe your child is at risk of harm from your co-parent, you should seek urgent independent legal advice. In some cases, the level of conflict between the parents can of itself be the cause of emotional harm to the child.

(f) how capable each of his parents, and any other person in relation to whom the court considers the question to be relevant, is of meeting his needs;

Parenting capacity is of course relevant, but be aware that in the vast majority of cases both parents will be deemed capable of meeting their children's needs. Huge leeway is given for differing parenting styles. This is not about choosing the 'better' parent, and Judges often bend over backwards not to imply one parent is more able than the other. The more likely outcome, in contested Court proceedings, is that a Judge will find that both parents can meet their child's physical and educational needs, but that their inability to shield their child from their own adult disagreements means they are both failing to meet their child's emotional needs.

(g) the range of powers available to the Court under this Act in the proceedings in question.

Perhaps an obvious point, but Judges can only make orders where they have been given the power to do so. So, issues which really relate to your relationship as co-parents are unlikely to be ones to which you will find a solution in the Courtroom.

So, what have the Courts said?

Children should normally have a relationship with both parents
Lord Justice McFarlane (who subsequently became President of the Family Division) in Re A [2015]:

> It is and should be a given that it will normally be in the best interests of a child to grow up having a full, real and entirely ordinary relationship with each of his or her parents, notwithstanding the fact that they have separated and that there may be difficulties between the two of them as adults.

Mr Justice Wilson (who subsequently became a Justice of the Supreme Court) in Re M [1995]:

> [it is a] fundamental emotional need of every child to have an enduring relationship with both his parents.

The Courtroom is not the place to resolve relationship issues
Lord Justice McFarlane in Re W [2013]:

> This case before us is one riven with very substantial difficulties. Both parents ... are human beings, each with benefits and detriments, capacities and incapacities to bring to the task of establishing a healthy relationship between their son and each of his two parents. The stand-off in the case is not one readily capable of resolution as a legal dispute with lawyers and Judges in a Courtroom. It is a problem of human relationships, and in the end it only will be resolved or ameliorated by a change in the key human relationship between the parents, assisted, one hopes, by the wider family ... They each have a responsibility now to look to each other, to look to their child, to see whether there are ways, despite the stand-off, despite the Court order, in which this boy can be brought up to have a favourable positive image of the absent parent ... It will not be easy. It will take both of them to understand and empathise with each other and to begin to meet each other even a quarter of

the way will be a step in the right direction. One hopes the wider family will assist them.

A child's views are important, but not necessarily determinative
Baroness Hale in Re D [2006]:

As any parent who has ever asked a child what he wants for tea knows, there is a large difference between taking account of a child's views and doing what he wants … But there is now a growing understanding of the importance of listening to the children involved in children's cases. It is the child, more than anyone else, who will have to live with what the Court decides. Those who do listen to children understand that they often have a point of view which is quite distinct from that of the person looking after them. They are quite capable of being moral actors in their own right. Just as the adults may have to do what the Court decides whether they like it or not, so may the child. But that is no more a reason for failing to hear what the child has to say than it is for refusing to hear the parents' views.

It is the responsibility of parents to promote each other in their children's lives
Lord Justice McFarlane in Re W [2012]:

Where parents separate, the burden for each and every member of the family group can be, and probably will be, heavy. It is not easy, indeed it is tough, to be a single parent with the care of a child. Equally, it is tough to be the parent of a child for whom you no longer have the day-to-day care and with whom you no longer enjoy the ordinary stuff of everyday life because you only spend limited time with your child. Where all contact between a parent and a child is prevented, the burden on that parent will be of the highest order. Equally, for the parent who has the primary care of a child, to send that child off to spend time with the other parent may, in some cases, be itself a significant burden; it may, to use modern parlance, be 'a very big ask'. Where, however, it is plainly in the best interests of a child to spend time with the other parent, then, tough or not, part of the responsibility of the parent with care must be the duty and responsibility to deliver what the child needs, hard though that may be.

Where there are significant difficulties in the way of establishing safe and beneficial contact, the parents share the primary responsibility of addressing those difficulties so that, in time, and maybe with outside help, the child can benefit from being in a full relationship with each parent ... the only interests that either parent should have ... in mind [are] those of each of their two children.

And, as a further example of how the Courts view your roles as co-parents in promoting each other to your children, here is the President of the Family Division again, Re H-B [2015]:

The responsibility of being a parent can be tough, it may be 'a very big ask'. But that is what parenting is all about. There are many things which they ought to do that children may not want to do or even refuse to do: going to the dentist, going to visit some 'boring' elderly relative, going to school, doing homework or sitting an examination, the list is endless. The parent's job, exercising all their parental skills, techniques and stratagems – which may include use of both the carrot and the stick and, in the case of the older child, reason and argument – is to get the child to do what it does not want to do.

The court will not 'micro-manage'

In the case of *T v S* [2013], the parents couldn't even agree where in Clapham Junction station they should 'hand over' their son. This is what the then President of the Family Division, Sir James Munby, had to say about their approach:

There is an appalling spectre lying ahead for these parents and, more particularly, their son. There seems to be a complete inability to do anything by agreement. There has been a distressing volume of correspondence between the parties and their solicitors. It is a feature which I am readily able to accept that virtually nothing is achieved by agreement. It does not follow from this that the solution is for the Court to embark upon the kind of further investigation that the father is suggesting. Unless the parents both recognise their responsibilities as parents, take account of the wise words of Mr. Justice Hedley, and adapt their behaviour accordingly, the consequences for the child caught in the middle of what a CAFCASS Officer described as a 'toxic relationship' hardly bear thinking about.

'If we do go to Court, what is the process?'

We may well have successfully put you off the Court process by now! But it's good to be informed about how the experience is likely to play out.

The first thing that many separating parents do not realize is that even if you go to Court, you may never see an actual Judge. Unless your case involves particular complexities, such as international elements or serious allegations of abuse, it will most likely be allocated to Magistrates. The majority of cases about child arrangements on divorce start this way. Magistrates are 'lay' people from the community who have been recruited and trained to hear cases. They are not lawyers. They will not usually have a legal background. They are unpaid. They are informed about the law and procedure by a Legal Adviser who will be sitting in Court with them, but it will be the Magistrates themselves who make the decisions about your children (whom they will not have met).

In terms of the Court experience, here are a few key pointers:

- There is no one size fits all if your case goes to Court. The process follows a framework set out by the Child Arrangements Programme.[6] Proceedings can become fairly drawn out, depending on the issues raised.
- The Court will expect you to have already engaged in some sort of out-of-Court dispute resolution process, such as mediation or the joint co-parenting service we offer at The Divorce Surgery, unless this is unsuitable for you due to issues of safety. At the very least you will need to have attended a

meeting, currently called a MIAM (Mediation Information and Assessment Meeting), to learn about what out-of-Court dispute resolution processes are available. The court will not process any application by you until you have attended such a meeting, or confirmed why you are exempt from attending. As we've already discussed, even after your application has been issued, the Court can of its own motion (and without your consent) adjourn the case if it considers you should engage further in out-of-Court dispute resolution.

• Once the Court issues your application, Cafcass, the Child and Family Court Advisory and Support Service, a public body set up to provide welfare guidance to the Family Court, will do some preliminary screening checks known as 'safeguarding'. This involves a very short telephone call with each of you. This will identify if there are any reported issues which would potentially make child arrangements unsafe, including for example domestic abuse or any other safety or welfare concerns. Cafcass will also cross-check with the police and social services. Cafcass then provides a short letter to the Court before the first hearing, setting out their view as to the way forward for your case.

Assuming you don't reach agreement, there are then three Court hearings (although in a complex case there could be many more):

1) The First Hearing Dispute Resolution Appointment (FHDRA)

A duty Cafcass Officer (not the one you spoke to on the phone) will usually attend the Court hearing to help you reach an agreed position. If you can't agree, the Court will then consider what further evidence it requires before it imposes final decisions on you both and your children. The Court may require a full report from Cafcass (known as a section 7 report), albeit these are rare in cases where there are no safeguarding concerns. If a Cafcass report is directed, the Cafcass Officer will set out their recommendations as to the arrangements for your child at the end of the report. Judges can depart from those recommendations, provided they have reasons for doing so. It is worth being prepared for the fact that if the Cafcass report is considered by the

Judge to be thorough and well prepared, it can be very persuasive. If they can afford it, some parents choose to pay for an Independent Social Worker to undertake the role of a Cafcass Officer, provided the Court agrees. This enables them to choose the identity and experience of the person undertaking the report.

In complex cases there may be a need to consider psychological or psychiatric assessments, or evidence from other third parties such as the police. But in many cases, where there are no safeguarding issues, just two parents who disagree about the arrangements for their children, the Magistrates will simply ask you both to set out in writing (in a witness statement) what Court Order you are seeking and why. You may also be directed to attend (separately) a Separating Parents Information Programme, a group session which focuses on the negative impact of parental conflict on children.[7]

2) The Dispute Resolution Appointment (DRA)

This is another opportunity which Courts build into the process to see if they can help you reach an agreement. If further evidence has come in (for instance a Cafcass report), this can be reviewed. Depending on the issues in your case, the Court may have listed the hearing to consider some of the short-term disagreements between you, such as the time you each spend with your children between now and the final hearing. If no agreement can be reached on your long-term disputes, the Court will list a final hearing.

3) The Final Hearing

This is the trial, the embodiment of the adversarial process. You will each try to 'defend' your respective positions and 'attack' the position of the other parent. Your written witness statements will stand as your evidence, but you can both be asked questions about what you say by the 'other side', which is called cross-examination. You may be representing yourselves, or you may choose to have solicitors and barristers representing each of you. If Cafcass has prepared a report, the Cafcass

Officer will also attend to give evidence, unless you both agree to their recommendations.

By its very nature, a trial is not about compromise. You will be passing the decision-making to a third party who has never met your child. At the end of the day (or sometimes after several days), the Magistrates or Judge will deliver their reasons in a judgment, and an order will be drawn up reflecting that decision, whether you like it or not.

In more complex cases, particularly where allegations of abuse are disputed, the Court may order a split trial (in effect two trials), where at the first trial, called a Fact-Finding Hearing, the Court just hears evidence on the disputed allegations (so what you each say did or did not happen) and decides what is more likely than not to have happened, and the second trial, which considers what is in your child's best interests, then uses that version of events as its factual basis, whether you each agree with it or not.

In terms of how long the process takes, the Courts were overwhelmed even before the Covid-19 pandemic, so delays can be significant. Our experience is that it often takes at least three months to get the first hearing listed, and if you go to final hearing you are unlikely to resolve the case in less than a year. If a Cafcass report is needed, that in itself usually takes about three months to produce.

It is worth bearing in mind what this means for your lives: you will be in litigation, and therefore in conflict with each other, for a prolonged period of time. Stress will build, making for the worst possible backdrop to co-parenting your child. The Court process really should be your last resort.

Final hearings are usually listed for a day, or sometimes more, but FHDRAs and DRAs are shorter hearings which are only listed for an hour. However, unless these are remote hearings (which are facilitated with the Court's own video service), the reality of the experience is that you will be in the court building for most of the day. Many Courts 'bulk list', which means they list several cases at 10 a.m. then several more at 2 p.m. Judges will normally call into Court the cases that are agreed first, so it can be a long wait, in rather dingy and run-down Court waiting rooms. Don't assume you'll have a private room or anywhere comfortable to sit.

'Who pays for the Court process?'

As a result of the Legal Aid, Sentencing and Punishment of Offenders Act 2012, legal aid is now unavailable for most parents who access the Courts following a divorce or separation, unless they are victims of domestic violence.

Budgeting for divorce is a really important place to start, and is highly achievable, unless you end up in the Court process. This is because the length of proceedings, and their cost, is then largely out of your control. In our experience from private practice, couples who end up in contested Court proceedings regularly spend five, and sometimes six, figures *each*. Almost nobody can budget for that, and the costs quickly snowball as the litigation drags on. Paradoxically, the longer proceedings go on, the more disillusioned parents become, but the less able they are to reach agreement, because all trust has broken down.

So, it's vital you go into Court proceedings with your eyes wide open as to how it can be funded. These are the main options:

You each pay your own solicitor and barrister out of your own savings

This is increasingly rare, because most people simply don't have enough savings to meet the costs, and also because often one parent may hold more savings than the other. It is worth being aware that, unlike other areas of law, family lawyers do not generally offer 'no win, no fee' payment plans, (and in any event in family litigation there are rarely 'winners' and 'losers').

One, or both of you, fund your respective costs with a litigation loan

This is a loan at a commercial interest rate which is secured against an asset which you are expected to recover at the end of the litigation, for instance the family home. This is an avenue which is open to you when it comes to any financial claims you may make, but is unlikely to be available in most cases about your children, because the Court isn't making orders about assets, so there is no easy route back to repayment for the lender.

One of you asks the Court to order that the other parent should pay your legal fees as well as their own, as they are in a better financial position than you

If one parent can demonstrate to the Court that they cannot fund legal fees, but the other parent is in a financial position to cover the costs of both sets of lawyers, Courts can and will make an order for them to do so, as it may well consider that it is in the child's best interests for each parent's position to be fairly and equally represented by lawyers (often referred to as 'equality of arms') and to ensure a fair trial. As you can imagine, if you are the parent funding both sides, this haemorrhaging of cash on two sets of lawyers can be extremely stressful, as the only way out of it is a negotiated settlement, which you alone cannot control.

You run into debt to fund the legal proceedings

You use personal loans and/or credit cards and borrow money from family and friends. This can be financially disastrous, and put extreme pressure on family relationships.

It's worth knowing too that costs orders (where at the end of a case the Judge orders one side to pay for the legal fees of the other side on the basis that one side has 'won') are rare in children proceedings. The starting-point is that you each pay your own legal fees.

What about ...? A few commonly asked questions, answered

'What if one of us wants to move away with our child?'

Divorce is often a trigger to re-evaluate your life. One of you may well want to move to be nearer family, or to follow a job opportunity you would not have considered when you were still together. Sometimes this involves moving to the next county, sometimes across the globe. Relocations (when one parent wants to move away with their child and the other parent disagrees) are often some of the hardest decisions for Family Judges to make. Sanctioning a child's move to Australia with one parent, against the wishes of the other parent, can be catastrophic in terms of the 'left-behind' parent's involvement in their child's day-to-day life. But trapping one parent in a location in which they no longer want to be, sometimes for a decade or more, can feel like a prison sentence to a parent who just desperately wants to move on with their life. These are extremely hard, binary choices.

The law in this area is now largely settled, in that a Judge is required to weigh up each parent's proposals as part of a holistic analysis in order to evaluate which is the outcome that best meets the child's welfare needs.[8]

These decisions are often very finely balanced. Each parent can usually make a strong case for their respective proposal, and it regularly comes down to the instinct of the Judge on the day and their assessment of the two parents in the witness box and the Cafcass Officer's recommendations. Because the decision has such life-changing consequences, the 'losing' parent will often be keen to appeal. So these sorts of cases can drag on, sometimes for years, with both parents and their children in limbo.

If you are in a situation where it is possible that at some stage one of you may want to relocate, talk about it together at the earliest opportunity. Bring in some expertise if you feel that would help you, in a joint forum if you can, and ensure that whatever expert you choose, be that legal, co-parenting, independent social worker or mediator, has experience in relocation. Listen to each other's perspectives and be open to finding a bespoke solution which could work for your family. We never cease to be amazed by the ability of co-parents to find the right outcome for their child even in the most challenging life circumstances if they both engage with the right mindset.

'Should I be pushing for 50 per cent shared care?'

No! Please don't obsess about percentages of time. Far, far too many parents get caught up in a hellish cycle of litigation over the difference between their child spending six, seven or eight nights with them a fortnight. It takes us back to the points we discussed in Step 5 – the Court process is in fact preventing you from seeing what's really important.

Think back to when you were in a relationship. Did you ever calculate the percentages you each cared for your child then? No. Could you tell us now? Most likely not, because caring for a child has all sorts of complexities which vary week to week. Do you count the time they are sleeping? What about when they are at school? What about all the time they are in your physical care but you are cracking on with work, or chores round the house, or browsing social media? It's a fool's errand trying to pin down quantity. What matters is *quality*. And knowing that you are your child's parents all the time, wherever they are. You don't stop being a parent when you go to work, or they go to school. *You're both parents 100 per cent of the time.* So know that a desire for equal nights, or majority nights, is likely to be much more about your insecurities, not what's best for your child.

It's really easy to get away from percentages. Assuming you're agreed that care needs to be shared in some way, start from your child's perspective. Look at their timetable each week. Some commitments are constant – school pick-up times, clubs, nursery. Look at your respective work and home commitments. Who can best do the pick-up on particular days? Are there particular activities that are 'your' thing with your child? If so, they're going to want to continue doing those things with you if it's feasible. Don't become fixated on the routine that was in place when you were all living under the same roof. Things are going to be different now. When it comes to weekends, many parents end up alternating, as that then gives them the freedom to do more and it's less to-ing and fro-ing for their children. But very young children might prefer to spend some time with each parent each weekend, even just for the short term. Be flexible. Recognize things will change. Aim to be in a space where you and your fellow co-parent can ask each other for help if work explodes, or you're unwell, or your child's unwell. Know that if you don't count nights, your children won't.

'What if I don't like what's in a Court Order? Can I just refuse to comply with it?'

Enforcement of Court Orders is a complex area which is outside the scope of this book. However, there are some fundamentals we would like you to know:

- Courts have a wide range of powers to encourage compliance with their orders, including requiring a Cafcass Officer to monitor compliance, ordering a parent breaching an order to undertake unpaid work (community service), pay financial compensation to the other parent if their actions caused financial loss, or even, for the most serious and flagrant breaches, be committed to prison.
- Ultimately, a Judge can change a child's living arrangements and move them from one parent to the other or even to foster care if they decide that the child's welfare demands this.

So the takeaway is this: don't breach Court Orders. Ideally, reach an agreement you can both live with and which affords the flexibility a Court Order simply can't provide.

'Should I push for an order that my child "lives with" me as opposed to "spends time with" me?'

The Court will usually first determine how your child's time should be apportioned between the two of you, before going on to consider how to 'label' the arrangement (so whether the order states that your child 'spends time with' one parent and 'lives with' the other, or 'lives with' each of you).

Far too many parents end up fighting over the label, when in reality the legal significance is minor (if you have a 'lives with' order you can, strictly speaking, take your child abroad for up to a month without the other parent's consent; however, in reality you are likely to have committed in the Court Order to give each other notice in advance of foreign trips, and in any event, unless you're fleeing an abusive situation, you should both know about any holiday plans which involve your child).

Parliament and the Courts have for years been trying to get away from these fights about labels. In 1989, the Children Act replaced the term 'custody' with 'residence' and 'contact'. These were in turn replaced in 2014 by 'spends time with' and 'lives with'. Sadly, this continues to be an issue which parents fight over. All we can say is what we tell the couples who come to see us: don't go to Court over a label.

What about parental alienation?

Cafcass defines 'alienation' as 'when a child's resistance/hostility towards one parent is not justified and is the result of psychological manipulation by the other parent'.[9] We weren't sure whether to say anything about parental alienation here. It's a huge, and highly divisive, topic, and if you're reading this book it's unlikely to be an avenue you're going down. However, we both know from past experience that these cases can start small, and often parents who end up being accused or accusing the other of 'alienating' their child could never, 12 months previously, have imagined ending up there. So this is really a word of warning.

Nearly every aspect of parental alienation (or 'implacable hostility to contact', as it is also called) is hotly contested. It is up for debate whether 'parental alienation syndrome' actually exists, and many independent social workers, psychologists and psychiatrists who work in this highly specialized area are seen, rightly or wrongly, as being 'for' or 'against' parental alienation. So the choice of expert, where one is needed, can be a minefield.

In 2018, the President of the Family Division delivered the keynote address to the Families Need Fathers conference. In it, he observed that whilst it was not important to determine definitively whether or not a 'parental alienation syndrome' actually existed, in some cases a parent could, either deliberately or inadvertently, turn the mind of their child against the other parent in circumstances where this was not justified. He observed, '… where that state of affairs has come to pass, it is likely to be emotionally harmful for the child to grow up in circumstances which maintain an unjustified and wholly negative view of the absent parent'.[10]

These cases start with a reluctance, and sometimes an outright refusal, by the child to see one of their parents. Everyone then searches for *why*. Sometimes the parents come up with two diametrically opposed answers to that question: one parent says that there is no good reason for the child's attitude and that it must be down to the other parent 'poisoning' the child against them. The other parent's position may be that, in fact, the child's views are their own and justified by the fact that they have been the victim of or witnessed abuse by the other parent. The Judge is left having to determine where the truth lies.

But not all cases are quite so stark, which is why we brought in the Mick and Jan case study (*for more, see below*). Many cases which end up in protracted and stalemated litigation start with a small slight, a missed cue, a breakdown in communication. If your child is crying when they see you together, or starts to express reluctance to move between your homes: talk about it. Don't assume they don't want to leave you or that the other parent has got them worked up. Get some co-parenting help, ideally from an expert who is qualified to speak to your child in an age-appropriate way and can explore what is going on. If we may venture an opinion in this hotly debated field, it is that the label 'parental alienation' may not always reflect the nuances on the ground. It is very rare indeed for one parent to bear all the blame and the other to be blameless. What you need is to engage with your child and each other, openly and without an agenda, to work through the issues that arise together.

JAN AND MICK

As you may recall from Step 5, Jan and Mick have a daughter, Lucy, who is 6 years old.

Jan is upset because Mick has moved out. Mick is very surprised by her reaction. He thinks space will do them both good.

They stop communicating with each other and each focus on what they feel is right for Lucy. For Jan, this means the stability of Lucy being largely in the family home with her and her nanny and seeing Mick on Saturday afternoons, but not staying overnight in his 'pokey' flat. Mick, on the other hand, thinks what Lucy needs is to see far more of him. He has secured a flexible working arrangement and proposes that Lucy spends three nights a week with him 'with immediate effect'. Jan stops replying to his emails, which she feels are bullying.

Lucy is, of course, caught in the middle. She now cries when she sees her parents together. Jan interprets this as meaning that Lucy doesn't want to leave her and isn't enjoying her time with Mick. Mick knows that once he gets in the car with Lucy and drives away, she is fine. So he thinks Jan must be causing the upset.

Mick instructs a family lawyer. He explains it has now been 9 months since the separation and Lucy has never stayed overnight with him. He doesn't want to let the situation drag on. On his instructions, his solicitor writes a letter to Jan, asking her to agree to a phased increase in the time Lucy spends with Mick, up to 3 nights a week in 3 months' time.

This letter from a lawyer is a huge shock to Jan, and throws her into a panic. Rather than considering the proposals, she feels under attack. She instructs her own lawyer and describes in detail the anguish she sees Lucy experience each week at handover. She feels Mick is bullying and is not the person she thought he was. She worries what might be behind Lucy's clear reluctance to go with him.

And so the stage is set. With every Court hearing and legal letter, Mick and Jan become more distant from each other. They no longer see each other as whole human beings, but as caricatures: the uncaring, cold father and the paranoid, over-anxious and possibly alienating mother. Lucy increasingly cannot cope with the emotional turmoil of handovers, and refuses to see her father at all.

Cafcass is brought in, then there are psychological assessments of both parents and Lucy. Many months go by. The financial cost is ruinous. Neither Mick nor Jan are functioning well at work or at home. Both are desperate to find a way through, but the damage to their relationship is such that it seems impossible.

Their positions have hardened. Mick now argues that Lucy should move to live with him, as Jan is incapable of promoting his position in Lucy's life. Jan says that Lucy should not be forced to spend any time with Mick, her views are her own and she needs to be freed from litigation without a Court Order for her to spend time with Mick.

So Lucy's parents' solutions are binary – neither can put forward a scenario in which both are actively involved in Lucy's life. And the Court is left to decide between two wholly undesirable outcomes.

We are conscious this is tough information to digest. But far, far too many separating parents launch into Court proceedings without realizing that it may in fact makes things much worse and not provide the resolution they so desperately seek.

What we want to do is empower you both with the knowledge that it is possible, and desirable, to resolve disagreements about your children together. You don't have to cede control to a Judge or Magistrate, who is, after all, a stranger and will almost never meet your child. No doubt you may be assisted with some expertise along the way, perhaps from a co-parenting expert, or a mediator, or a shared lawyer. But they will be working to your *joint* agenda.

OVER TO YOU ...

Setting the agenda

Now is a good time to set the agenda. What are the areas upon which you are agreed and where are you struggling?

You will have been through the parenting plan in Step 5. Use that as your base, and also consider the checklist below. If you can, go through it together. If not, make your own notes separately and then meet to discuss them:

- How are you going to support each other to share your children's care:
  - » During term time?
  - » During half-terms?
  - » During school holidays?
- How are you going to manage important holiday periods such as Christmas, Easter, Eid, Diwali and Passover?
  - » Think about what your children would want – would it be important to them to see you both on the day? Or would they rather have the excuse to celebrate twice, i.e. with each of you separately?
  - » Think about logistics: do you want to be transporting your children between you on those days? How do your plans fit in with wider family plans? Are there particular events with cousins which your children would be sad to miss?
- Start thinking about birthdays:
  - » An easy one is your own – your children no doubt will want to spend time with each of you on your birthdays, so think how that can be managed, depending on whether it falls on a school day or a weekend/holiday. The same goes for Mother's Day and Father's Day. Think about the small things (which are often really the big things). Can you each commit to help your child get a card and present for the other parent's birthday and Mother's/Father's Day?
  - » Your children's birthdays:

» Is there a way for you both to spend time with your children on their birthdays? Or is there another solution which would be better for your children? Remember, of course, on this of all days they shouldn't be thinking about how their celebration impacts their parents.

» What about their party? Who will organize it? Will you both attend?

» What about presents? Can you coordinate? The more you think about these small logistics in advance, the less there will be to trip you up later on.

- Foreign holidays:

  » Can you agree you are both happy for the other parent to take your children abroad?

  » Are there any countries you would not want the children to visit for safety reasons?

  » Can you agree to give each other notice of any foreign trip (a common agreement is to give at least a month's notice of the planned trip and then at least two weeks before provide flight, contact and accommodation details). Remember if your child is away and you see some disaster on the news, you will want to know how to communicate to be sure they are safe.

- Communication:

  » Between your child and each parent when they are in the care of the other:

  » This will depend on your children's ages and your approach. Some parents simply say that their children can call or Facetime the other parent whenever they want, whilst others want to restrict the use of technology and so suggest particular times on particular days. Some children aren't big talkers and find forced Facetime or phone calls a real drag. There is no right answer, but find something that works for your children, and both of you, and remember to be flexible – the needs of human beings don't always fit into set schedules.

  » Between each other:

  » When are you going to talk about your children together? Some parents find a monthly coffee, scheduled in the diary, is a good way to cover any issues which arise.

» In front of your children:
» How is your behaviour with each other in front of your children? Is it horribly awkward? If so, they will no doubt have noticed. Are there ways you can try to break the ice yourselves? If not, consider going to see a co-parenting expert together, even just for one session, to get things in better shape.

- School choices:
  » Are you approaching any important decisions which will affect your children, for instance school choices?
  » Have you exchanged information about the relative merits of the schools you like, for example reports from Ofsted, and/or the Independent Schools Inspectorate?
  » Could you visit the schools together, or separately, to ensure you are both fully informed?
  » Have you each written down a list of preferences and seen where they coincide? Does this produce an outcome which you can both accept?

Quite simply, we want you to reach the point at which you know (a) where you're agreed and (b) where you aren't. You can then decide what professional support you need to resolve your differences. Are these legal issues or relationship issues? For many parents, there will be some of each. If so, prepare a list of the points that need help from a co-parenting expert and those that need legal advice. By honing down the 'brief' to your experts, you can then clearly define their role and hopefully agree a budget for the work. Again, this is you running your own separation and retaining control.

There is no timeline for this step. Remember constructive discussions take time and that's fine. What you want to avoid is long periods of time when the discussions aren't constructive and you are actually in conflict. If that is starting to happen, recognize it and get professional help.

Sometimes families and friends can derail you during these sensitive discussions. In Step 9 we're going to consider how to manage your support network so they boost you and don't undermine the progress you're making. But first, we'll look at reaching a financial agreement.

EXAMPLE OF A COURT ORDER

In the Family Court
Case no: [Case number]
sitting at [Court name]

The Children Act 1989
The child[ren]
[Name of child] _____ [Girl]/[Boy] _____ [dob dd/mm/yy]
[Name of child] _____ [Girl]/[Boy] _____ [dob dd/mm/yy]

Order Made by [Name of Judge] Sitting in Private at a Final Hearing on [Date]

The parties and representation:
- The applicant is [name], the mother, represented by [barrister/solicitor name]

The respondent is [name], the father, represented by [barrister/solicitor name]

Important Notices
Confidentiality warning
The names of the child[ren] and the parties are not to be publicly disclosed without the court's permission.

Child arrangements orders warnings
This order includes a child arrangements order (the part of the order setting out living arrangements for a child and about time to be spent or contact with another person). If you do not do what the child arrangements order says you may be made to do unpaid work or pay financial compensation. You may also be held to be in contempt of court and imprisoned or fined, or your assets may be seized.

It is a criminal offence to take a child out of the United Kingdom without the consent of everybody with parental responsibility unless the court has given permission.

While a child arrangements order is in force in relation to a child nobody may:

- cause the child to be known by a new surname
- remove the child from the United Kingdom

without the written consent of every person with parental responsibility for the child or leave of the court.

However, this does not prevent the removal the child from the United Kingdom by a person named in the child arrangements order as a person with whom the child is to live for a period of less than one month.

Recitals

Issues

- The parties have agreed that:
  - » the child[ren] will live with [name] [until further order];
  - » the child[ren] will spend time with [name] as follows: [insert];
  - » [insert].
- The issues that the court needed to decide were as follows:
  - » with whom the child[ren] should live;
  - » whether they should spend time with the other parent and, if so,
  - » how often;
  - » whether there should be overnight stays and longer stays;
  - » whether it should be supervised or supported;
  - » whether it should be limited to indirect contact;
  - » the child[ren]'s education;
  - » the child[ren]'s names;
  - » holidays or travel plans;
  - » proposed relocation by [name] with the child[ren] to [insert].

The Court Orders
Jurisdiction
- The court declares it is satisfied it has jurisdiction in relation to the child[ren] based on habitual residence.

Live with order
- The child[ren] shall live with [name] [as follows: [insert]].

Contact order
- [Name] must make sure that the child[ren] spend[s] time or otherwise [has]/[have] contact with [name] as follows: [insert details].

Contact directions and conditions
- The following conditions apply to contact:
  » handovers at the start of contact will be at [place] and [name] must [collect]/[deliver] the child[ren];
  » handovers at the end of contact will be at [place] and [name] must [collect]/[deliver] the child[ren];
  » handovers at the start and end of contact will be at an agreed public place covered by CCTV cameras [namely [place]];
  » the parties must ensure that [no other adult] [name] accompanies them to handovers;
  » any party delayed for a handover must let the other know immediately;
  » handovers will be facilitated by [name];
  » communication between the parties must be confined to issues concerning the child and must only be by text message/email. The telephone numbers/email addresses of the parties are [insert];
  » a 'contact handover book' shall be used to note any matters of concern of importance which one party needs to tell the other. The book is to be used solely for communication about contact arrangements and the health and welfare of the child[ren] [and must not be used to criticize or verbally abuse the other parent]. The book must be passed from one

party to the other at contact handovers and must be brought to court
on each occasion the parties attend.

Specific issue order

- [Name] must
  - » return the child[ren] to the care of [name] immediately [upon service of this order];
  - » make sure that the child[ren] attend school at [name of school];
  - » make sure the child[ren] [is]/[are] known by the last name [surname];
  - » deliver the child[ren]'s passport[s] to [name] by [date];
  - » [insert].

Prohibited steps order

- [Name] must not
  - » remove the child[ren] from the care of [name] or any person or institution (including any nursery or school) to whom that party has entrusted the child[ren]'s care, nor instruct nor encourage anybody else to do so, other than for the purpose of contact agreed in writing or ordered by the court, in which case the child[ren] must be returned promptly at the end of each such contact period;
  - » allow the child[ren] to live at a different address than [address];
  - » remove the child[ren] from their current school;
  - » remove the child[ren] from the United Kingdom;
  - » allow the child[ren] to be known by a different surname than [surname];
  - » [insert].

Costs

There is no order for costs.

STEP 8

|||||||||||||||||||||||||||||||||||||||||||||||||||||||||||||||||||||||||||

REACHING A FINANCIAL AGREEMENT

|||||||||||||||||||||||||||||||||||||||||||||||||||||||||||||||||||||||||||

'How do we reach a fair deal?'

In Step 4 we looked at the Court's powers to redistribute your property and income between you upon divorce. In Step 6 we looked at financial disclosure and establishing what you have. So far, so good. But now what? It's time to look at *how* the law reallocates resources based on the disclosure you have provided.

So there is going to be some law over the next few pages. Please try not to worry excessively, though – this isn't something to be feared, nor do you need a cold towel wrapped around your head! This is your – all of our – law, as voted for and enacted by our representatives in Parliament and developed by our Judges. It is there to serve you and your family, to protect each and both of you, and your children if you have them, and to provide some tramlines for your discussions. Try not to think of this as some dusty academic exercise – above all, family law is designed to be pragmatic. There is rarely one 'answer' to these cases, but lots of possible answers. We hope this step can guide your approach.

The social history of the twentieth century means that the law relating to family finance remains heavily focused on married relationships. We think the law relating to unmarried couples is seriously underdeveloped, but we are where we are in that respect and there will have to be legislative change before any meaningful advances can happen. Inevitably, therefore, this discussion focuses mainly on separating married couples, although there are some similarities for unmarried cohabitees with children, which we'll point out towards the end of the step. Family law does not have very much at all to say about unmarried couples *without* children, as we have already seen.

'If I've read this, do I still need legal advice?'

Yes, probably. What follows is not going to give you all the answers for your particular circumstances. But it should at least demystify the process and enable you to understand what is relevant and what isn't.

Bear in mind that if you want a Court Order to sort out your finances, as part of that process you'll also be resolving your legal claims against each other. There are many important aspects of the divorce process which need not involve lawyers at all, but this isn't one of them. For most of us, agreeing a divorce settlement is likely to be amongst the biggest surrenders or gains of assets we make in our lifetime, so it needs to be done right. But as ever, be careful how you access your legal advice. Keep an eye on cost, and work together if you can. You don't necessarily need lawyers on hand throughout, but you will want their help when the time is right.

'So, what is the law actually trying to do?'

The overarching idea, as you might expect, is to divide your resources *fairly*, according to the laws set down by Parliament, as developed and interpreted by Judges.

But what on earth is meant by *fairness*? That sounds unhelpfully woolly ... Fair to whom? Judged by what criteria? As the House of Lords (as we used to call the Supreme Court) put it back in *White v White* [2000]:

> Everyone would accept that the outcome on these matters, whether by agreement or Court order, should be fair. More realistically, the outcome ought to be as fair as is possible in all the circumstances. But everyone's life is different. Features which are important when assessing fairness differ in each case. And, sometimes, different minds can reach different conclusions on what fairness requires. Then fairness, like beauty, lies in the eye of the beholder.

To state the obvious, reasonable people may reasonably disagree about what's fair, particularly in the throes of divorce. So might those tasked with imposing a solution, if one cannot be agreed (i.e. the Judges).

Many separating couples instinctively feel that dividing their resources 50–50 is right. But equality is only one aspect of fairness. If your former partner is in full-time well-paid employment but you are the main carer for four children under the age of 10, are not in work and have no savings and no mortgage capacity, then an equal division of the equity in the family home may not be very fair at all. So it depends.

A discretionary system

Perhaps the first point to make is that, as with the law relating to children, the law is highly discretionary in this area. This means that individual Judges work within a broad framework of rules and expectations set by Parliament, within which they have enormous freedom to do what they think is right.

There are pros and cons to this, as you might expect. On the plus side, Judges can tailor the outcome to suit the needs of every individual family they see. If it is fair, for example, to award ongoing spousal maintenance at £1,500 per month for the next five-and-a-half years because at that point your youngest child will be in secondary school and you'll be able to work full time, then that is what the Court can and will do. You can have a bespoke outcome. By contrast, in other countries Judges are prevented from doing that because maintenance orders can only be for the short term. So in principle a discretionary system can sometimes suit the needs of individual families better.

There is also the wider point that this in-built flexibility allows legal outcomes to develop in tune with social developments. Family law is a living, breathing organism that reflects our evolving social priorities. Outcomes for divorcing women in particular are very different today than they were when the current legislation was introduced in 1973, all made possible within the existing structure (imperfect as it undoubtedly is).

The flip side of having a bespoke system is that outcomes are not always particularly obvious. This can make cases harder to settle, with all the added stress and expense that brings. Other than in the most clear-cut of cases, even the most eminent lawyers will struggle to tell you what your ongoing maintenance liability will be, simply because different Judges will come to different conclusions. Where something as nebulous as fairness is the goal, unpredictability will follow.

There is ongoing debate in England and Wales as to how to balance these arguments. Reform has been proposed in the form of Baroness Deech's Divorce (Financial Provision) Bill,[1] which aims to simplify outcomes more along the lines of the system in Scotland. Whether it will have that effect, if it passes, remains to be seen.

Recap as to the Court's powers

As we've seen in Step 4, the Court has very wide powers indeed to divide up your jointly owned assets between you, and what's more, to award the assets of one of you to the other and vice versa. Capital, income and pensions can all be reallocated between you. It's important to recognize that such powers are necessary because the ceremony of marriage itself does not affect the ownership of assets. Tying the knot doesn't mean your worldly possessions are also united, at least not under English law.

Identifying the Court's powers is the easy bit, however. But how and when are they used?

HOW DOES THE COURT EXERCISE ITS POWERS?

The historical context is fascinating, if completely outside the remit of this book! Suffice it to say, the availability of financial provision for *women* on divorce has developed over time. Although continuing spousal support in one form or another has been available since at least 1857, capital provision of any sort only arrived in the second half of the twentieth century.[2] And as we saw in Step 6, there is still a great deal to do to ensure an equitable division of pension resources upon divorce.

The rules of the game these days are set by the Matrimonial Causes Act 1973 (we'll call this the 1973 Act from now on). That piece of legislation provides guidance as to matters the Court must take into account, as well as a couple of pointers as to what we should all be aiming to achieve, but the detail of exactly how the law is supposed to deliver fairness has been left overwhelmingly for Judges to develop …

But first, the legislation.

List of factors the Court has to consider – the 'section 25 criteria'

In deciding how to exercise its powers to reallocate resources, the Court *must* consider 'all the circumstances of the case' and also specifically the criteria set out in section 25(2) of the 1973 Act:

> *(a) the income, earning capacity, property and other financial resources which each of the parties to the marriage has or is likely to have in the foreseeable future, including in the case of earning capacity any increase in that capacity which it would in the opinion of the Court be reasonable to expect a party to the marriage to take steps to acquire;*

So, as we saw in Step 6, the Court looks at *all* your resources, including those you will have in the foreseeable future. If it considers you are under-utilizing your earning capacity, it can take this into account when it comes to considering your need for maintenance/your ability to pay it.

> *(b) the financial needs, obligations and responsibilities which each of the parties to the marriage has or is likely to have in the foreseeable future;*

Again, as we say in Step 6, an assessment of each of your 'needs' is central, as are your liabilities, such as tax, credit card debt, personal loans, ongoing responsibility to pay school fees and so on.

> *(c) the standard of living enjoyed by the family before the breakdown of the marriage;*

The Court has to take into account the marital standard of living, but it would be a mistake to think the law simply aims to replicate that going forward. As has been said earlier on, it is rarely possible to do so once two households are established, with two sets of outgoings.

(d) the age of each party to the marriage and the duration of the marriage;

This is often vital context in the assessment of what's fair. Equality of outcome may be far less relevant in the case of a retirement-age couple following a short second marriage than it might be for a couple in their early fifties who've been married for 30 years.

In assessing the duration of the marriage, the Court will invariably include any prior period in which you lived together, provided that period led seamlessly into married life.

(e) any physical or mental disability of either of the parties to the marriage;

Whether this adds anything much to the mandatory assessment of 'needs' described above might be in doubt. But clearly any physical or mental disabilities and any costs of care have to be borne firmly in mind when it comes to delivering overall fairness.

(f) the contributions which each of the parties has made or is likely in the foreseeable future to make to the welfare of the family, including any contribution by looking after the home or caring for the family;

Without discriminating between financial and other types of contribution, for example taking primary responsibility for childcare, has either of you made some contribution which it would be appropriate to recognize in the outcome? This won't be relevant unless there are sufficient resources available to meet needs and after that a surplus left over.

(g) the conduct of each of the parties, if that conduct is such that it would in the opinion of the Court be inequitable to disregard it;

The test is not whether either of you thinks there has been relevant poor behaviour, but whether the Court thinks it would be 'inequitable to disregard' such behaviour. This is in practice a very high threshold indeed. We'll look at this further below, but this is wholly irrelevant for most couples.

> (h) in the case of proceedings for divorce or nullity of marriage, the value to each of the parties to the marriage of any benefit which, by reason of the dissolution or annulment of the marriage, that party will lose the chance of acquiring.

In this context, beware the loss of any pension benefits suffered by a dependent spouse upon the granting of Decree Absolute (or under the new no-fault divorce rules, a Final Order).

As keen students of the Form E will note, the evidence you are obliged to supply to the Court is designed to ensure all of the above criteria can be addressed.

'Besides the list of things to consider, does the 1973 Act say anything else about the approach we should be taking?'

Yes, but not very much at all. There are really only two pieces of guidance given:

- Focus on children

  > It shall be the duty of the court in deciding whether to exercise its powers [...] and, if so, in what manner, to have regard to all the circumstances of the case, first consideration being given to the welfare while a minor of any child of the family who has not attained the age of eighteen.[3]

'Children of the family' refers to any child brought up and maintained within the marital household, so can encompass those from previous relationships if they were treated as children of the family.

- The Court must impose a 'clean break' where possible

Whenever the Court uses its powers to reallocate resources, it must also:

> Consider whether it would be appropriate so to exercise those powers that the financial obligations of each party towards the other will be terminated as soon after the grant of the decree as the court considers just and reasonable.[4]

And, even where the Court is specifically ordering ongoing spousal maintenance, it must:

> Consider whether it would be appropriate to require those payments to be made [...] only for such term as would in the opinion of the Court be sufficient to enable the party in whose favour the order is made to adjust without undue hardship or the termination of his or her financial dependence on the other party.[5]

The clear idea here is that the Court should try to ensure that the parties do not remain financially linked to each other unless this is unavoidable. In practice, whether this is possible or not will depend greatly on the sufficiency of the resources available for division.

As we shall see, where ongoing spousal maintenance is ordered, it should only be for as long as necessary to permit the recipient to 'adjust without undue hardship'. Some hardship is acceptable, so it is a question of degree.

Beside these two important – but in reality fairly narrow – requirements, Judges and Courts have more or less been left to get on with it.

SO, WHAT HAVE THE COURTS SAID?

Over time, Judges have attempted to flesh out the broad framework provided by the 1973 Act in order to provide more consistency and predictability for divorcing couples. Here are some of the major principles which guide the Courts in England and Wales in 2022 in relation to the reallocation of resources upon divorce:

Discrimination between spouses is not permitted

White v White [2000], Lord Nicholls:

> If, in their different spheres, each contributed equally to the family, then in principle it matters not which of them earned the money and built up the assets. There should be no bias in favour of the money-earner and against the home-maker and the child-carer.
>
> [...]
>
> a judge would always be well advised to check his tentative views against the yardstick of equality of division. As a general guide, equality should be departed from only if, and to the extent that, there is good reason for doing so. The need to consider and articulate reasons for departing from equality would help the parties and the court to focus on the need to ensure the absence of discrimination.

As an aid to ensuring non-discrimination between spouses, the Court should cross-check its anticipated outcome against 'the yardstick of equality' before reaching a firm conclusion. It is perfectly acceptable to order an unequal division of resources, provided there are good reasons to do so. But diminishing the contribution of the home-maker compared to that of the 'breadwinner' is not one of them.

Three possible reasons to reallocate resources between spouses

In *Miller, McFarlane* [2006], the Court undertook a root and branch review of the philosophy and law relating to the division of resources upon divorce and concluded that in English law there are essentially three possible justifications for reallocating one party's resources to another: (1) Needs (2) Sharing and (3) Compensation. Their unifying theme is that

> each is looking at factors which are linked to the parties' relationship, either causally or temporally, and not to extrinsic, unrelated factors, such as a disability arising after the marriage has ended.
>
> Lady Hale

With a handful of exceptions, 'Compensation' has not really prospered as a rationale in the years since. The idea is that where one party has given up well-paid employment in order to fulfil mutual choices made within the marriage – caring for children being the most obvious example – then the law should recognize that sacrifice and the consequential impact on earning capacity many years later. It is essentially conceived as a guard against discrimination. But subsequent cases have stressed the difficulty in establishing and then assessing claims brought under this heading. How is the loss to be established and then quantified? Should the Court weigh in the balance the non-financial benefits in giving up paid work, and if so, how? And, as we shall see, can't you get to more or less the same result by application of the Needs principle anyway?

So, what about Needs and Sharing?

Needs

This is by far and away the most common rationale deployed to justify the division of resources. In summary, the law tries to stretch what's available to ensure each of you (with first consideration being given to the welfare of any minor children) is securely housed and in a position to meet your daily living costs. A division of pension assets to provide for retirement is also key. In *Miller, McFarlane* [2014], Lord Nicholls put the reasoning like this:

> This element of fairness reflects the fact that to a greater or lesser extent every relationship of marriage gives rise to a relationship of interdependence. The parties share the roles of money-earner, home-maker and child-carer. Mutual dependence begets mutual obligations of support. When the marriage ends, fairness requires that the assets of the parties should be divided primarily so as to make provision for the parties' housing and financial needs, taking into account a wide range of matters such as the parties' ages, their future earning capacity, the family's standard of living, and any disability of either party. Most of these needs will have been generated by the marriage, but not all of them. Needs arising from age or disability are instances of the latter.
>
> In most cases the search for fairness largely begins and ends at this stage. In most cases the available assets are insufficient to provide adequately for the needs of two homes. The court seeks to stretch modest finite resources so far as possible to meet the parties' needs.

The Court is specifically required to consider needs under the 1973 Act. But in such cases, there is no room to consider other competing aspects of the section 25 criteria, for example, contributions: who funded the acquisition of the family home, or the later extension, whether one or other of you had a modest pot of savings at the outset, and so on. Every penny is accounted for in meeting needs, present and future. There is nothing left over.

Doing so can result in outcomes which are miles away from equality. It may be necessary to divide up the equity in the family home very unequally if, for example, one party has a significant mortgage capacity and is in a position to borrow, whereas the other party is not and will therefore need to be mortgage-free. In such cases, the law takes a wide view of what is fair.

Sharing

Sharing cases (sometimes referred to as 'equal sharing' cases) are those where there remains a surplus of resources left over after both parties' needs are met. In this context, the origin of the resources to be divided and the duration of the marriage can become crucial. In *Miller, McFarlane* [2006], it was explained like this:

> This 'equal sharing' principle derives from the basic concept of equality permeating a marriage as understood today. Marriage, it is often said, is a partnership of equals [...] This is now recognised widely, if not universally. The parties commit themselves to sharing their lives. They live and work together. When their partnership ends each is entitled to an equal share of the assets of the partnership, unless there is a good reason to the contrary. Fairness requires no less. But I emphasise the qualifying phrase: 'unless there is good reason to the contrary'.

In a sharing case, where there is a surplus of resources once needs are met, the Court will try to distinguish between 'matrimonial property' and 'non-matrimonial property' as a guide to working out the ultimate division.

We'll explore this more below, but for now it's enough to know that matrimonial property is ordinarily shared equally, whereas non-matrimonial property is only reallocated when justified by needs.

'Matrimonial property and non-matrimonial property – what are they?'

Despite not being mentioned anywhere in the 1973 Act, the distinction between matrimonial and non-matrimonial property has come to be amongst the most fundamental principles underpinning the law in this area. As the Court in *Miller, McFarlane* explained:

> There is a real difference, a difference of source, between (1) property acquired during the marriage otherwise than by inheritance or gift, sometimes called the marital acquest but more usually the matrimonial property, and (2) other property. The former is the financial product of the parties' common endeavour, the latter is not. The parties' matrimonial home, even if this was brought into the marriage at the outset by one of the parties, usually has a central place in any marriage. So it should normally be treated as matrimonial property for this purpose. As already noted, in principle the entitlement of each party to a share of the matrimonial property is the same however long or short the marriage may have been.
>
> The matter stands differently regarding property ('non-matrimonial property') the parties bring with them into the marriage or acquire by inheritance or gift during the marriage. Then the duration of the marriage will be highly relevant. [...]
>
> In the case of a short marriage, fairness may well require that the claimant should not be entitled to a share of the other's non-matrimonial property. The source of the asset may be a good reason for departing from equality. This reflects the instinctive feeling that parties will generally have less call upon each other on the breakdown of a short marriage.
>
> With longer marriages, the position is not so straightforward. Non-matrimonial property represents a contribution made to the marriage by one of the parties. Sometimes, as the years pass, the weight fairly to be attributed to this contribution will diminish, sometimes it will not. After many years of marriage, the continuing weight to be attributed to modest savings introduced by one party at the outset of the marriage may well be different from the weight

attributable to a valuable heirloom intended to be retained in specie. Some of the matters to be taken into account in this regard were mentioned in the above citation from the White case. To this non-exhaustive list should be added, as a relevant matter, the way the parties organised their financial affairs.

Working out what is and is not matrimonial property in a sharing case can be a very significant undertaking in itself. It is not always possible to draw a firm dividing line between the two – for example, if one of you owned shares in a fledgling company prior to your relationship which have become valuable during the course of a long marriage. In such a case, it may (or may not, depending on practicality and proportionality) be necessary to try to obtain expert evidence as to the value of the shareholding at the date of the marriage and also now.

The family home is normally treated as matrimonial property, and is usually shared equally (unless needs say otherwise, of course, or there are important other circumstances, such as an ancestral home which has been in one spouse's family for generations).

'Needs' are overwhelmingly the justification for ongoing spousal maintenance

In the years since the 1973 Act, there have been repeated attempts to work out a principled basis for the division of *income*, as opposed to capital. The settled position nowadays is that ongoing spousal maintenance is almost always determined by reference to needs alone.[6] An earning capacity cannot be regarded as an asset capable of being shared. Whilst the decided cases have kept open the possibility of compensation working to enhance the assessment of needs, there are hardly any examples of this happening in practice.

'But how do all these abstract concepts actually work in practice?'

Scatliffe v Scatliffe [2016]:

> In an ordinary case, the proper approach is to apply the sharing principle to the matrimonial property and then to ask whether, in the light of all the matters specified [in section 25(2)] and of its concluding words, the result of so doing represents an appropriate overall disposal. In particular it should ask whether the principles of need and/or of compensation, best explained in the speech of Lady Hale in the Miller case at paras 137 to 144, require additional adjustment in the form of transfer to one party of further property, even of non-matrimonial property, held by the other.

So the present state of the law in England and Wales means the constituent parts of a financial case go something like this:

1. Ascertain your present and future resources, obtaining any necessary valuation evidence along the way.
2. Distinguish between any matrimonial and non-matrimonial property.
3. Is sharing of the matrimonial property, normally equally, sufficient to meet the needs on both sides?
4. If not, identify the shortfall and reallocate resources as required, including from non-matrimonial property if need be.
5. Check if the proposed division of resources is fair overall.

'And what is the Court process?'

If you can't agree on the division of your finances and make an application to Court for a Family Judge to resolve it for you, there are four key stages. These are interesting to note because they follow the set pattern you should both be adopting in trying to agree the arrangements away from the Court arena:

- You need to demonstrate that, at the very least, you have explored ways of resolving your disagreement away from Court (*see* Step 2). At the time of writing, this means the person applying needs to attend a MIAM (Mediation Information and Assessment Meeting). The direction of travel is that these requirements are only going to become tougher, in line with the judicial and Government objective of making Court the place of absolute last resort.
- You need to do your best to agree your financial picture (*see* Steps 3 and 6). What this means in the Court arena is that you each have to complete a Form E, exchange it and then ask each other written questions about any areas which require further clarification. You may need an expert report to value certain assets (*see* Step 6). These disclosure issues are ones which are considered at the first Court hearing, the First Directions Appointment (FDA). If all these points can be navigated and agreed, normally neither of you needs to attend the hearing, provided you or your lawyers lodge an agreed order setting out the next steps.
- You need to do your best to reach agreement yourselves. To help you with this, the Court requires you to attend a second hearing, a Financial Dispute Resolution Appointment (FDR). This is a settlement hearing at which a Judge will tell you both what they would consider a fair result, in an effort to get you both to compromise. This is similar to other steps you can take, such as sharing a lawyer to advise you both from the start. However, the FDR comes much later down the line, often six to nine months after you have made the Court application, so your positions can be quite entrenched by that stage, and the cost (both emotional and financial) will be high. If you don't settle at the FDR, all offers made during that hearing remain confidential, and you will always be allocated a new Judge, so that you start any final hearing with a clean slate.
- If you still cannot agree, the last stage is the final hearing. You will have prepared written witness statements which will stand as your evidence, but you and any witnesses can all be asked questions about what you say by the 'other side', which is called cross-examination. You may be representing yourselves, or you may choose to have solicitors and barristers representing each of you. By its very nature, a trial is not about compromise. You will be

passing the decision-making to a third party. At the end of the day (or sometimes after several days), the Judge will deliver a judgment and an order will be drawn up reflecting that decision, whether you like it or not. In terms of how long the process takes, if you go to final hearing it is likely to take longer than a year, and sometimes much longer. During that time there will be conflict between you (or you would not have ended up at a final hearing) and it is almost always a stressful and costly process.

WHAT ABOUT ...? A FEW SPECIFIC POINTS OF INTEREST WHEN IT COMES TO DIVIDING FINANCES

Pre-nuptial agreements ... What are they and do they work?

In the last 20 years, English Courts have begun to pay more and more attention to 'prenups' whereby the parties seek to agree in a legal document before their marriage how financial issues will be resolved if they later separate. See *Radmacher v Granatino* [2010]:

> The court should give effect to a nuptial agreement that is freely entered into by each party with a full appreciation of its implications unless in the circumstances prevailing it would not be fair to hold the parties to their agreement.

Prenups work. But in order for a prenup to stand the best chance of being upheld, ensure:

- It is signed free of any undue influence, fraud or misrepresentation by either party.
- There has been full disclosure of both parties' resources.
- Each has a full understanding of the implications of the prenup.
- Each has taken independent legal advice on its terms.
- It is signed not less than 28 days prior to the wedding/civil partnership.
- It meets each party's needs at the point of divorce.

As the law currently stands, even where a prenup provides 'the answer', you will still need a Court to approve a consent order reflecting its terms, if you want to resolve your financial claims against each other.

How relevant to the financial outcome is it if one of us is in a new relationship?

Beware the 'remarriage trap'! If you remarry (or enter into a civil partnership), you will not be able to apply in the future for financial provision under the 1973 Act from your former spouse, other than in relation to pension-sharing orders. And if you are already the recipient of Court-ordered spousal maintenance from your former husband or wife, the legal requirement to make those payments ceases automatically upon your remarriage. There *may* be certain other things you can do under other statutes, but these are outside the scope of this book, and you can of course continue to bring more limited claims in respect of any children you have together, as we explain later on in this step.

Assuming you have not remarried or entered into a civil partnership, though, the mere fact that you're in a new relationship is not relevant unless the relationship is a cohabiting one. If it is, the Court may take into account the extent to which it would be reasonable for that cohabiting partner to be contributing to the shared expenses of the household (i.e. not whether that partner *is* contributing … but whether they *ought* to be), both in income terms and possibly also in capital terms if, say, you intend to purchase property together in the future.

So in short, cohabiting partners can impact the assessment of needs, but do not affect an award based on sharing.

'Conduct' ... Is behaviour ever relevant?

The origins of conduct as a relevant feature in the allocation of resources go back to the days when a wife's award could be reduced if she were judged to be at fault for the demise of the relationship (which says a lot about the origins of divorce stigma). Fortunately we have moved on, to the point where the law requires the Court to ignore allegations of poor behaviour, unless it would be 'inequitable to do so'. To reach that standard, the Courts have held that the conduct complained of must be 'both obvious and gross',[7] sometimes described as having a 'gasp factor' – for example, a sexual assault on a child of the family, or a jealous husband disfiguring his spouse. Therefore, for the vast, vast majority of separating couples – happily – conduct can be completely ignored.

More common are complaints of 'financial misconduct', where, for example, one party wishes to argue that matrimonial resources have been deliberately or recklessly spent or moved, so that there is now less to divide. But the Court starts from the premise that each of you, even within marriage, is entitled to do what you want with your own money. You'll want legal advice if you think financial misconduct applies to your situation.

Child maintenance

Responsibility for determining maintenance for children (as opposed to spousal maintenance) primarily lies with the Child Maintenance Service (CMS). However, the Family Court does retain the power to make orders for child maintenance in certain circumstances, including in particular where:

- the payer's gross income exceeds £156,000 per annum and the CMS has declared that it does not have jurisdiction for that reason, known as a 'maximum assessment'

- an order is sought for expenses in connection with a child's disability
- an order for the payment of school fees is sought
- one parent lives outside the UK

When deciding on an appropriate sum, the Court will ordinarily use the CMS formula as a starting-point, although it may depart from it as it sees fit.

IBRAHIM AND AISHA, A 'NEEDS' CASE ...

Ibrahim and Aisha, aged 44 and 40, married in 2007 and now have a boy and two girls, aged 16, 12 and 8. They have recently decided to divorce. Ibrahim has moved out to a rental property for the time being, but the children go to stay regularly and Aisha is supportive of this. It is agreed that the children will continue to have their main base with Aisha.

Ibrahim works full time as a web designer, earning £60,000 gross pa. Aisha works part time as a bookkeeper, earning £18,000 gross pa. The marital standard of living was modest but comfortable.

The four-bedroom family home is worth £465,000, but is subject to a mortgage of £160,000. Allowing for costs of sale at 3 per cent, there is equity of £291,050.

Besides this, there are cash savings in an ISA of £10,000, two cars (Ibrahim's is subject to finance) and the contents of the house. Ibrahim's pension has a CEV of £180,000, whereas Aisha has no private pension at all.

The couple go together to see a specialist family law barrister and afterwards agree:

- The family home should be sold and the mortgage redeemed.
- Each party needs to be housed in three to four-bedroom accommodation, including the costs of purchase, Stamp Duty and moving costs. Aisha needs to be close to the current primary and secondary schools attended by the children. Ibrahim has more flexibility when it comes to location and a fourth bedroom. Based on local estate agents' particulars, Aisha will need a

housing fund of £310,000, including moving costs and Stamp Duty. The equivalent figure for Ibrahim is £275,000.

- Aisha can reasonably borrow a maximum of £75,000 and Ibrahim can borrow £220,000.
- The remaining proceeds of the sale of the family home will be divided 80 per cent (£235,000) to Aisha and 20 per cent to Ibrahim (£56,000).
- Ibrahim will retain the savings, and each will keep one car.
- Each will now be able to rehouse at the level they agree is appropriate. But Ibrahim's monthly mortgage payments will be much more than Aisha's.
- Ibrahim's pension should be subject to a pension-sharing order to provide for equality of income to each party in retirement, assuming each retires at age 67 (the ordinary date for receipt of state pension). The costs of implementing the pension share should be met equally.
- Having visited https://www.entitledto.co.uk/, Aisha thinks she will now be able to claim Universal Credit of almost £7,000 pa, plus Child Benefit of a further £2,000 pa.
- Ibrahim will pay child maintenance (using the CMS calculator as a starting-point) of £8,000 pa.
- Ibrahim will pay 'nominal spousal maintenance' to Aisha until the youngest child completes her full-time secondary education. Note: Ibrahim does not actually pay anything (the order might require him to pay, say, £1 per annum), but this aspect of their agreement keeps open Aisha's maintenance claims for herself in case circumstances require higher payments to be made in due course, for instance if she loses her job, until she secures another.

It is plain that an equal division of the matrimonial property will not meet Aisha or the children's needs. So the division of resources is slanted – heavily – in Aisha's favour.

Ibrahim and Aisha considered in particular whether it would be right to award Ibrahim further capital once the children are independent and Aisha no longer requires such a large property. However, in the end, Ibrahim agreed he was likely to be earning much more than Aisha at that stage, as Aisha's earning capacity would continue to be affected by her childcare commitments for the foreseeable future, if not forever.

Once his higher mortgage payments are factored in, Ibrahim cannot afford to pay spousal maintenance as well as the child maintenance. So they have agreed instead simply to keep Aisha's claims open in that respect, in case payments become desirable in due course. There will be a clean break once their youngest child finishes school.

||||||||||||||||||||||||||||||||||||||||||||||||||||||||||||||||||||||||||||||||||||||||||||||||||||||||||||||||||||||||||||||||||||||

This is not the only way to resolve this case. Different Judges will have different views on the extent of each party's housing and income needs, and that will drive the outcome. And consideration of overall 'fairness' will impact on whether Ibrahim receives a further lump sum in due course.

It is key to work out how much of each party's income will be disappearing in mortgage costs each month, based on the proposed capital division.

MOIRA AND AMANDA, A 'SHARING' CASE ...

Amanda and Moira are aged 39 and 36 respectively. They met and fell in love 10 years ago, when both were living and working in London. At that stage, Moira owned a flat in Bristol, which she rented out, using the income to pay down the large mortgage, and she has continued to do so.

At the point of their civil partnership, each was earning well – Amanda at a property consultancy, earning £70,000 gross pa, and Moira as a junior accountant at a good firm on £50,000 gross pa. Both earn considerably more now.

During the course of the civil partnership, they bought a property in their joint names, and a few years later a second investment property nearby, also in joint names. It was a stretch, but they could afford the mortgage repayments from their joint incomes, taking the view that they were investing for their future. Neither put money into a pension.

Amanda never had anything to do with the Bristol flat. She regarded it as 'Moira's affair' entirely, as did Moira.

Over time, they realized that they disagreed about whether they wanted to have children or not and this became a huge issue for them. The relationship sadly foundered.

They agree:

- Each can reasonably meet their own income needs from within their own resources, so there is no reason for either to pay the other maintenance. They agree to a clean break.
- The family home and second investment property will clearly be regarded as matrimonial property and therefore susceptible to equal sharing. Just as clearly, Moira's flat is non-matrimonial property.
- If equal sharing of the matrimonial property meets Amanda's needs, then that is the end of it. There is no obvious justification for awarding her any share of Moira's non-matrimonial property.
- But if equal sharing of the matrimonial property does not meet Amanda's needs (unlikely as that might be), then she might be awarded such share of Moira's non-matrimonial property as would be required to do so – subject, of course, to Moira's needs also being met.

UNMARRIED COUPLES WITH CHILDREN

The statutory equivalent of s.25 of the Matrimonial Causes Act 1973 for unmarried couples with children is known as 'Schedule 1', shorthand for 'Schedule 1 of the Children Act 1989'.

We've looked at the powers the Court has in Step 4, but as a recap, they are significantly less wide than for married couples. The object of the exercise here is not to reallocate resources fairly, but only to the extent necessary to provide for children.

As to how the law wants those powers exercised, consider paragraph 4 of Schedule 1 of the Children Act:

4 [1] In deciding whether to exercise its powers under paragraph 1 or 2, and if so in what manner, the Court shall have regard to all the circumstances including –

Again, what follows are mandatory considerations. The Court *must* take them into account.

[a] the income, earning capacity, property and other financial resources which each person [...] has or is likely to have in the foreseeable future;

This is in similar terms to s.25(2)(a) of the Matrimonial Causes Act 1973, albeit there is no requirement on the Court to consider whether one of the parties could earn more.

[b] the financial needs, obligations and responsibilities which each person [...] has or is likely to have in the foreseeable future;

Again, this is couched in similar terms to the matrimonial legislation.

[c] the financial needs of the child;

This is a stand-alone consideration here, unlike in the matrimonial legislation, and underlines the specific purpose of the exercise under Schedule 1.

[d] the income, earning capacity [if any], property and other financial resources of the child;

This is rarely a relevant feature in practice, but can in principle be relevant to the assessment of needs.

(e) any physical or mental disability of the child;

This is also obviously relevant to needs.

(f) the manner in which the child was being, or was expected to be, educated or trained.

This is relevant to the assessment of needs, including the timescales over which support is required.

It is interesting to see what *isn't* in the list above, compared to the matrimonial legislation. Although the Court must consider 'all the circumstances', there is no express requirement at all for the law to consider: (i) the length of the relationship; (ii) standard of living during the relationship; (iii) 'conduct'; (iv) 'contributions'; or (v) the ages or health of the parties. As we saw in Step 6, when you give financial disclosure in a Schedule 1 case, you use Form E1, which is shorter than the Form E used by divorcing couples, largely because it omits any reference to these additional matters.

Principles applied by the Court

As with the matrimonial legislation, there is little by way of explicit direction in Schedule 1 itself. So again the Courts have tried to provide some predictability. The major considerations are:

- The welfare of the child will be a constant influence on the outcome.
- A child is entitled to be brought up in circumstances bearing some relationship to the paying parent's resources and standard of living.
- The Court must guard against unreasonable claims brought by a parent with a disguised element of providing for that parent's benefit rather than that of the child.

Unless and until legislative reform is brought forward, the Schedule 1 regime will continue to be less comprehensive and less generous than that in place for divorcing couples. This does *not*, of course, prevent unmarried couples from making whatever financial arrangements suit them.

||||||||||||||||||||||||||||||||||||||||||||||||||||||||||||||||||||||||||||||||||||||||||||||||||||||||||||||||||||||||||||||||

OVER TO YOU ...

||||||||||||||||||||||||||||||||||||||||||||||||||||||||||||||||||||||||||||||||||||||||||||||||||||||||||||||||||||||||||||||||

Reaching a financial agreement

Hopefully the above gives you some pointers to what is and isn't relevant in your own situation and will enable you to identify the issues on which professional advice will be helpful.

It's time to start working out what you already agree on and what needs more thought. Here are some suggestions to get you started:

Establishing your resources
- Are you satisfied that you understand each other's financial position and that full and frank disclosure has been given?
- Do you have a solid idea of what you each can borrow, if need be?
- Have you remembered to establish any tax liabilities?
- If you are not satisfied as to the level of financial disclosure given, can you establish the gaps and try to agree a timetable for filling them?

Establishing your future housing needs
- Do you agree what sort of housing you'll both need for the future and what it's likely to cost? Have you actually seen what is available first hand, rather than simply through online estate agents' particulars? Can you imagine your former partner (and, if you have them, your children) living in the types of property you are suggesting, and vice versa?

- If purchasing a property is intended, don't forget the Stamp Duty Land Tax and other costs of purchase, such as solicitors' fees, survey fees, etc.
- If renting, don't forget ground rent, service charges, etc.

Income
- Do you agree what level of income you will each need going forward, bearing in mind the needs of your children? Can you imagine living within the budget you are proposing for your former partner, and vice versa?
- Can you each meet your income needs from your own earning capacity, or is help likely to be needed? If it is, for how long?

Pensions
- Check you haven't forgotten about or ignored pensions.

Sharing cases
- If you think your combined resources exceed what is required to meet each of your needs, do you have an understanding of what is matrimonial property and what is non-matrimonial property?

Now is the time to take legal advice tailored to your specific circumstances. Do your research carefully and find out what is available to suit your budget. If funds are limited, consider in particular when you take legal advice. Joint early legal advice can be very effective at reassuring each of you that your respective positions will be protected, but still keep your interests aligned, and give you the answers you need to take forward your settlement discussions.

STEP 9

||||||||||||||||||||||||||||||||||||||||||||||||||||||||||||||||||||||||||

MANAGING OUR FRIENDS AND FAMILY

||||||||||||||||||||||||||||||||||||||||||||||||||||||||||||||||||||||||||

'How do we get the support we need from our friends and family?'

This step is about managing your friends, family and work colleagues so you get the support *you* need. Frankly, you've got enough to be dealing with, so we've written this for your network to read. At the right time, you can thrust it in their hands and leave them to it. Feel free to read it too, of course, but remember how those around you behave is not down to you, and if they fail to give you what you need you can absolutely side-step them for a while. Your well-being, and that of your family unit, is paramount right now.

OK, friends and family, hello! This step is for anyone who knows someone going through a divorce or separation. Given that 42 per cent of UK marriages end in divorce,[1] pretty much everybody knows somebody who is navigating this change.

A help or a hindrance?

You can be either, and many people slip into being one or other simply by virtue of their preconceptions and unconscious biases. We're here to help you make an informed choice about the way you behave and the impact it has.

If you have a close friend or family member going through a divorce or separation and turning to you for guidance, or as a shoulder to cry on, whether you like it or not you are going to play an incredibly important role in how that divorce turns out.

In the thousands of divorces in which we have advised, both in Court and at The Divorce Surgery, we have seen, time and again, how supportive family members can be the difference between a couple negotiating sensibly, and making the necessary compromises, or becoming entrenched and embittered.

So, no pressure! But please do take some time to mull over what we are about to say, and think before you speak.

The backdrop you need to counteract

Say the word 'divorce' out loud. Can you think of a single positive connotation? No. And yet there are over 100,000 couples in England and Wales navigating this every year.[2] Blame Henry VIII, but we are conditioned, by centuries of bad press, to view divorce a 'a bad thing'.

Let's go back to basics. Can you force a person to fall in love with another? Clearly not. So can someone stop themselves falling out of love? Equally, no. Which is why blaming one partner or the other is so utterly pointless and unfair. Neither of us has ever come across some-one getting divorced 'on a whim'. Divorce is the product of months, sometimes years, of soul-searching and (at times deeply hidden) unhappiness. No one should expect to be happy every day, but equally nobody deserves to be relentlessly miserable.

So let's start from this premise: divorce isn't *necessarily* bad. It may be one of the best decisions your friend makes – for themselves, their former partner and any children they have. Because it gives them all another shot at happiness.

Why conflict is damaging

One of the many problems with adversarial litigation is that the process dehumanizes families. Watch a TV courtroom drama, or read a reported case, and you will see, at the very top:

Smith v Smith

But it's not *Smith v Smith*. It's really:

Human being v Human being

Family v Family

Person you once loved more than anyone v Person you once loved more than anyone

If you had a blank sheet of paper and had the freedom to devise a process by which separating couples could navigate the decisions surrounding the division of their finances and arrangements for their children, we doubt very much you'd suggest the adversarial one that our Family Justice system imposes. And that's coming from two signed-up members: as family law barristers, we have worked within the system for decades. But, from the get-go, it implies that one person is right and the other is wrong. That there will be a winner and a loser. In actual fact, in the vast majority of cases, what you have is two adults desperately trying to work out how their family and their finances will work after divorce. They are searching for answers, whilst the adversarial process is working to identify the issues that divide them.

This is what we want all separating couples to know, from the moment they decide to separate:

- That they both need to provide for themselves and any children financially. There is going to be a finite amount of money to go around. How their needs are met, and their resources are shared, can involve some hard choices. They may well, instinctively, reach perfectly rational but diametrically opposed views about what is fair. That's normal. So they'll need some financial and legal advice to inform them about what fairness in their situation looks like. Then they can reach an agreement. If they follow that path, *they never have to meet a Judge, or step inside a Courtroom.*

- If they have children, *they are both still parents 100 per cent of the time*. When one parent goes to work, or drops their children at school, or goes on a solo holiday, they don't stop being a parent because their child isn't in their physical care. The same applies to divorce. You're still a parent 100 per cent of the time. You're still a family 100 per cent of the time. You're just reconfigured. Many couples have a much better co-parenting relationship once they can let go of the part of their adult relationship that wasn't working. So, divorce can lead to happier, healthier adults, and happier, healthier children. Parenting following divorce involves the same logistical decisions as parenting during a marriage or relationship. Who can do school pick-ups on which days? Who manages which sporting commitments? These logistical choices don't need to be loaded with the concept that one or the other person will be 'less of a parent', depending on how the time is allocated. They will still *both* be parents *all the time*. And if they can agree the arrangements, there is no role for the Courts to play at all.

Now of course there are situations where the protection of the Court system is urgently needed: cases involving domestic abuse or conceal-ment of assets, or those where genuinely novel points of law are raised. But these situations arise only for a small minority of couples, thankfully. If your friend is in that situation, please tell them to get independent legal advice as soon as possible.

For the vast majority of separating couples, contested Court proceedings are avoidable if they approach their divorce in the right way.

And in case you still have a romantic notion that Court proceedings may provide some vindication for your friend, or 'closure', know this: there are no 'winners' or 'losers' in family litigation. Judges bend over backwards to make sure no one feels they have won, because they know how damaging that message can be for the wider family dynamic. In the vast majority of cases, Judges have no interest in who was to blame for the breakdown of the marriage, or what happened in the past. They are focused, in a very practical way, on the future: who will live where, how will that be funded, how are the children's needs to be met.

And don't underestimate the damaging impact months, sometimes years, of stressful litigation will have on your friend and, if they have them, their children. Research by the Nuffield Foundation in 2019 found that Court proceedings *in themselves* can cause emotional harm to the adults and children involved. The study found that 38 per cent of all separating couples in England and Wales ended up in adversarial Court proceedings over the arrangements for their children. Given the damaging mental health impacts of such conflict on families, the conclusion was that a public health response was needed.[3]

And now a word on the professionals working in this field. From the outside looking in, you may assume that family lawyers thrive on conflict. We don't. You become a family lawyer because you want to help people at a time of personal turmoil. The reason we set up The Divorce Surgery was because we felt there had to be a way for couples to share impartial legal advice so they understood how the law would apply to their family situation without being pitted against each other. It was also, selfishly, a way for us to feel that we were helping people, rather than facilitating a process which might be ultimately causing them harm. And we're not the only ones – there are many other family lawyers out there promoting different initiatives with the same goal of keeping couples out of Court.

If you want to know more about the impact of conflict on family lawyers, read the powerful and deeply moving essay a respected and very senior family law barrister specialising in child protection, Ian Griffin, wrote to and for the profession when he was dying of cancer.[4] It's the most extraordinary read, and please do read it in full if you get the chance (*the link is in the Notes and the Resources*), but here are some extracts:

> Every professional that acts and makes decisions in family law becomes part of the very fabric of the family law world; the family law barrister, solicitor, magistrate's clerk, magistrate, District Judge, the Circuit Judge, the High Court Judge and the Appellate Court Judge all make up this wonderful but difficult world. I consider that this 'world' in which we act, although profoundly rewarding, is also inevitably dangerous to our health.
>
> We change our holidays, we miss our children's school and life events, we work when barely capable through illness and often personal grief, we commit totally to our clients and we put the clients before our families and of course our own health. We often neglect those who love and support us to the point that it ruins our close relationships. We deal with the most awful of subject matters, a world most extreme and excoriating on one's physical, emotional and psychological inner person.
>
> Ultimately, in my view, we are all burnt and we are all scarred to a lesser or greater extent by what we do. There is no escape. We love what we do. We do good and sometimes great things. But we are inevitably hurt by what we do and what we are.
>
> ... My view is when are dealing with any human beings in our practice the default position is that we must view it is an UTTER privilege to do so. Whomsoever they are they put their world into YOUR HANDS at the most frightening of times.
>
> But, in my view, this is where the danger to you and me arises. Through toxic stress. I am quite sure my Cancer has a toxic stress-related element regarding causation.

But we MUST DO WHAT WE DO, the rule of law demands we exist.

The clients need us all, that is Barrister, Solicitors and Judges alike. We are involved in saving children, saving families and sometimes saving lives. Judges make the most difficult of life-changing decisions. We love what we do. But it is us and it is our way of being. We cannot stop what we do. It is like an addiction. What we do can be and is extraordinarily rewarding on a daily basis. Every day is different. We 'work' in a rarefied and privileged world, but our own hurt is an inevitable side-effect.

But we all pretend to have the defence to this hurt. We pretend not to care. We have open and overt cynicism (guilty as charged). We develop the darkest of senses of humour (guilty as charged). We drink too much alcohol, the 'care case medicine' to soothe our injuries. But in the end the relentless tsunami of subject matter will get to you. There is no defence. We all pretend to be hard as nails, but look into yourself and look at and out for friends.

You are all suffering from significant harm.

It might help to take a moment to reflect on this. If professionals within the field find it this stressful to represent their clients within adversarial Court proceedings (which we undoubtedly do), just imagine the stress for the couples involved and any children.

So it should be no surprise to learn that the most senior Family Judge in England and Wales, the President of the Family Division, is urging couples not to come to Court. He has made the issue of how to enable separating parents to navigate their child arrangements together, outside the Courts system, one of his top priorities.

The direction of travel is clear: in the next five to ten years it will become completely normal to expect a divorcing couple to navigate their divorce, and any advice they need, together. The Courtroom battle will, happily, become the anomaly, and should be avoided unless there really is no other way.

It's *not* about tactics

We can hear your response already: 'Well, that's all very well, but I want to make sure my friend/daughter/brother isn't out-manoeuvred by their spouse. Everyone says divorce is about tactics: who has the best lawyer, who stays in the family home, who has ready access to the bank accounts. Now is not a time for trust. It's a time to prepare for battle.'

One thing is clear: your friend will need legal advice. There are issues which may mean urgent protective legal steps must be taken, particularly in international families where there is a choice over the country in which the divorce should proceed. In cases of abuse, your friend will need urgent protection.

But in the vast majority of cases, those early pre-emptive steps don't influence the overall outcome, they simply dictate the kind of divorce you are going to have. If you start, from the get-go, on the assumption that you need to fight, then a fight is what you'll get. You'll make choices which are incendiary, such as freezing bank accounts, or limiting your children's time with the other parent, or changing the locks. Immediately it's two warring factions, with no middle ground.

But we encourage couples to start thinking about where they will end up. What will a Judge do at the end of the day? Let's consider that, together, from Day One. Don't waste your time clinging on to the family home if it's going to need to be sold and the mortgage payments are crippling you. At the very early stages of divorce, couples are usually in a state of shock and fear. And fear can lead to bad choices. But you (and we) can help your friend find a way out of the fear by empowering them with knowledge. And if couples can gain that knowledge together, from an impartial source, all the better.

So what does this mean, in practical terms, for you? Well, first and foremost, don't support the fear and tactics narrative. Encourage your friend to sit down with someone and understand the finances. How much is there to go around? If child arrangements are an issue, encourage them to get co-parenting advice. Talking to children about divorce is hard, and there are great professionals out there who can help both parents deal with it in the most child-focused way. Above all, encourage your friend to approach divorce as a shared problem to overcome with their former partner. The best way to navigate it fairly, without sky-high legal fees or months of conflict, is to reach an agreement both can live with. So start there.

You don't need to choose

When couples separate, their friends can be put in an invidious position. You may well have liked both of them, but been closer to one. Now you feel you have to make a choice. Which sucks.

But really, you don't. If you want to remain friends with both, you can. In fact, by making that choice early and telling your friends about it, you'll become someone valuable when the divorce is over: a neutral party. Because there is life after divorce. And, unsurprisingly, your friends will want to move on. So being surrounded by people who, themselves, invested emotionally in the divorce drama may be rather unappealing.

Don't play the blame game

When a friend is going through divorce, of course your instinctive reaction is to protect and support them. It's awful to see people who you love going through a hard time, and the knee-jerk reaction is often to find someone to blame. Sadly, in a divorce scenario, there's an obvious culprit. But please try not to fall into that bear trap.

You may think that what your friend wants to hear is lots of ex-bashing. How you never liked her/never thought she was good enough for him/always mocked his jumpers. Your friend may encourage this, and may seem to find it hilarious over a glass or three of wine. But after you've all gone home, that conversation is actually just going to make your friend feel worse.

One of the most corrosive aspects of divorce is the feeling that you have wasted a huge chunk of your life with the wrong person. That this whole period has been a failure, and time that you will never get back.

But that's not true. Getting divorced doesn't mean you made the wrong choice, or have bad judgement. You probably made the right choice at the time. Just because people change as they grow older and move apart doesn't mean they were never close, or never right for each other. By demonizing the ex, you are reinforcing the message that your friend made the wrong choice, which won't help them process the relationship breakdown well or give them hope for the future. And isn't hope what they need?

Say something nice – nobody else will

Which is why focusing on the positives, however counter-intuitive it may feel, is actually crucial. Yes, your friend's other half may have behaved like an idiot in the last 18 months, but there were some fun times before that. Remember them, even just to yourself. It will help you remember you are dealing with a whole person, and not just a caricature.

This is, of course, all the more important if your friend has children with their former partner. Co-parenting is a life-long partnership, regardless of whether the marriage lasts. It is going to cause emotional harm to your friend, and their children, if the other parent becomes the enemy. Give them permission to recognize their former partner as a decent parent. Lead by example. Encourage compromise – if the other parent wants to swap contact weekends for some reason, use that as an excuse to plan a fun night out, rather than making an administrative diary change into the personification of everything that is wrong with that person. Where you can, dial things down, rather than revving them up.

Remember divorce is still hard

As much as you try to perk up family and friends, it's also important to recognize that divorce involves emotions which are painful and raw. In the Instagram age of 'perfection', it's easy to slip into a dynamic where you fail to acknowledge that it's normal to feel sad, and to enable those around you to share negative feelings without immediately being told how to 'fix' them.

This is a concept psychologists call 'toxic positivity'. As David Kessler, a grief expert and author, has explained, 'Toxic positivity is positivity given in the wrong way, in the wrong dose, at the wrong time.'[5] And we all do it. Sometimes from our own awkwardness around other people's sadness, at other times because we don't know what else to say, or maybe simply because we don't have the time for the proper conversation, so we just instinctively shut it down with a coffee mug ditty: 'It'll be OK!' or 'I believe good things are around the corner!' or 'Let's focus on the positive!'

And the reason why this is so unhelpful, and counter-productive, is because the negative emotions need to be acknowledged, and lived in, and processed, or they won't be released. And if they aren't released, they'll just keep recurring. As Natalie Dattilo, clinical psychologist at Brigham and Women's Hospital in Boston and instructor of psychiatry at Harvard Medical School, says, 'Think of emotions as a closed circuit. They have to go somewhere, so they come back up, like Whack-a-Mole.'[6]

Difficult emotions are a part of divorce. So don't dismiss them. Acknowledge them. Talk them through. Then, gently, when you feel your friend is ready, try to bring in hope and optimism, rooted in the reality of their situation (rather than just announcing they shouldn't feel bad because at least they don't have cancer/live in a war zone).

Of course that means we are all walking a tightrope! But it can be done. Really it's the difference between encouraging hope for the future and just offering relentless positivity which gives no opportunity for feelings of grief or anger to be processed and released. Above all else, we want divorcing couples to be able to navigate divorce, and the swirl of emotions surrounding it, without being channelled into a blame narrative, which can act as an amplifier to feelings of anger and loss. Instead, let's all aim to give them an outlet for the release of those negative emotions, which is so needed to make room for a hopeful future.

Deal with your own emotions in your own time

Do you yourself feel angry, or betrayed, or let down by the divorce? If so, that's completely normal. When people we care for make decisions we don't expect or understand, it can be hard to rationalize. If you held up a couple as being your definition of a 'happy marriage', it can be a crushing blow, and bewildering, when it all falls apart. But you do not know, and will never know, what was happening in that relationship and how it was making those two people feel. The only objective fact you can possibly know is that, whatever your perspective, or your friend's perspective, the marriage clearly wasn't working for both of them.

Recognize that your feelings need to be processed in your own time, away from your friend. It's not going to help them one jot to be loaded with your feelings of hurt, or a two-dimensional analysis of why the relationship didn't work out. They will have a much more nuanced understanding, which they may never share with you. They may be anxious about how to justify a decision to forgive, or move on, due to worry about how *you* may react. Your job is to help them navigate *their* emotions, and to shield them from your own. That way you can morph, playdoh-like, into whatever support they need, without presuming to dictate the emotional agenda.

Are your views influencing their settlement?

This is crucial. You want the best for the people you love. Of course you do. And, as we've already discussed, being caught in a prolonged and expensive legal battle isn't going to be in their best interests. You're going to be an expert in knowing how to perk them up along the way and give them that crucial emotional support, but please be honest with yourself: you are not a legal expert. Even if you're a lawyer in another practice area, please don't spend five minutes reading some case law and decree you know what you're talking about in their case. And even if you are a family lawyer, you should know you can't possibly offer impartial advice to someone you know personally, as the objectivity just goes, which is why none of us do it.

So please don't announce what you think the financial settlement should be, or how your friend and their former partner should manage the extremely sensitive and personal choice of arranging the care of their children.

Time and again we see cases where the block to settlement isn't the couple themselves, but rather the fear of how to *justify* it to family members or friends. It seems extraordinary, doesn't it, but the power of peer endorsement and social networks is huge.

The best way to demonstrate this is through a case study:

GLORIA AND MARVIN

Gloria and Marvin are both in their mid-forties.

They have three children between the ages of 7 and 12.

Both started their careers at large accountancy firms. They were at the same level of seniority when Gloria got pregnant with their first child.

The burdens of parenthood forced them to take some tough decisions about how they would manage career and home. Gloria resigned from her job to stay at home full time. Marvin pressed on and has done well, although he has not yet reached partnership.

They live in London and have a comfortable lifestyle, although the costs of housing, school fees and day-to-day living have meant that they have no savings and a very large mortgage to service.

So the blunt point – and this applies to very many couples – is this: they can only just afford to run one household. Running two is going to involve considerable changes in lifestyle.

But divorce isn't a decision driven by maths. Couples separate because they are unhappy and because the relationship that once brought them joy is now a barrier to future happiness. So for Gloria and Marvin, as for many separating couples, the economic fallout has been an unwelcome discovery.

Unfortunately, they failed to recognize it for what it was: a shared challenge to overcome. Instead of talking to each other, and working together, they turned to those around them. This had a pivotal influence on their divorce.

Marvin spoke to a work colleague, Tim, who had had a long and acrimonious divorce. The whole office knew about it, and had partly lived through it, so Marvin thought he would be a good person to speak to, as he would obviously know a lot about divorce. Tim emphasized, repeatedly, that Marvin needed to 'protect his pension' and 'capitalize maintenance so he could get a clean break'. He recommended his own solicitor, who he said had been a 'pitbull' and 'wiped the floor with the other side'.

Pausing here: Tim, of course, is not an expert on divorce. All he can talk about is his own divorce. And given that that divorce took two years and cost Tim £250,000 (a figure he doesn't share with Marvin), it's highly debatable whether the aggressive approach he instructed his legal team to take really paid off.

Tim also has a completely different financial position from Marvin. He is more senior at work, has a partner-level pension scheme which is much more valuable than Marvin's, and has significant savings. The tax implications of sharing Tim's pension were complex, and it made sense, from a tax perspective, for him to keep more pension and his former wife to retain more capital. They had significant savings, such that his former wife's maintenance could affordably be capitalized. But Marvin knows none of this. He just knows (a) he needs to 'protect' his pension, (b) clean breaks are good and (c) he needs to approach this as a fight.

So Marvin is now not only burdened with a negotiating position which is completely unachievable, but also the peer pressure of a senior colleague who will be checking in on him. Tim will do this to be kind and supportive, but for Marvin, each time he makes a concession, he needs to think not only how to justify it to himself, but how he will explain it over a pint to Tim.

What about Gloria? She is inundated with advice. Her divorce becomes the key topic of conversation at every school coffee morning. She is told she needs to stay in the family home, get a 'joint lives maintenance order', and be cautious about offering Marvin overnights with the children 'in case it sets a precedent'. Gloria is utterly at sea. But overwhelmingly she feels this is about protecting her interests, and her role as a parent.

Gloria and Marvin have each entrenched themselves. It's almost inevitable now, before either has even taken legal advice, that this divorce is going to be long, painful and expensive. Because there will be mutually exclusive agendas. And Gloria and Marvin's separate solicitors, and subsequently barristers, will be tasked with achieving the unachievable. And this won't become clear to the lawyers until several months down the line, as Gloria's team will not have Marvin's financial disclosure, and vice versa, until they have exchanged their Forms E. Which usually takes weeks and sometimes months.

And all the time Gloria and Marvin have a drip-feed of frankly unhelpful narrative from those around them. Unsurprisingly, they aren't talking to each other about the divorce at all. Gloria thinks Marvin's position that she should be able to support herself financially within months so that he can have a clean break is wholly unrealistic (which it is) and also fails to acknowledge the sacrifices she made in giving up her career 12 years ago. Marvin cannot believe Gloria is pushing to remain in the family home when it is so obviously unaffordable (and he is right about that), and is growing increasingly anxious that she is 'playing games' with the children and won't allow them to enjoy a full relationship with him.

Behind the scenes, their separate lawyers are advising them to settle. But they aren't listening any more. They are convinced of the merits of their own arguments. And ultimately their lawyers have to follow their instructions, whatever their advice as to the prospects of success.

And so Gloria and Marvin end up in Court proceedings over both the division of their finances and arrangements for their children. It is financially ruinous, and the amount they spend on legal fees means they both have to move, not only to more modest homes, but to a cheaper area. Marvin doesn't get a clean break and he has to share his pension. The family home is sold by order of the court, despite Gloria's protestations, and she gets spousal maintenance, but only for a seven-year term until she can build her earning capacity again.

Not a good ending for anyone. What could Tim and Gloria's friends have done differently? Well, a few things:

- Recognized that their own divorce experience was going to be of limited value. What Tim said to Marvin really illustrated that he was still caught in the trauma of his own divorce. All he could really have said to help him would have been: 'I had a dreadful divorce which went on for years and cost me a fortune. I can't comment on what the right outcome would be for you, because I don't know your finances, but I can say get good advice and if there's a way to avoid an expensive and drawn-out battle, take it.'
- Gloria's friendship group could also have parked the legal advice and instead focused on emotional support and empathy for her as a person, without judging Marvin. She could have done with some nice distractions, and a laugh.
- Free from the fear-mongering, Gloria and Marvin might just have been open-minded enough to sit down together and look at their finances. Maybe visit a financial adviser together. Maybe even get some shared legal advice. That way, they could have quickly identified the limitations of what their combined financial resources could achieve. Instead of seeing their divorce as some highly tactical game of chess in which one wrong move would doom them forever, they could have identified that it was a life change to navigate together.

So, having freaked you out entirely about how your input could set things off on the wrong track, here's a few final tips to help you set the right tone for your friend.

No one wants their life to be a soap opera

Take a step back and analyse how much time you spend as a friendship group talking about this divorce. If it's most of the time, consider what you can do to change that. As much as your friend might appear to want to talk about their divorce all the time, it's not healthy, and won't help them move on if it's the single item on the agenda at every meet-up.

Also, it's awful to feel that you're the failure in your friendship group, the one who couldn't quite make things work. But divorce isn't a failure but a life change, one of several we will go through during our lifetime. And it doesn't mean that everything that went before was a mistake. A crucial role you can play is to reinforce this message. Make your friend realize that divorce is both normal and really not that bad. Put it in perspective (without, of course, dismissing it entirely). You can acknowledge it is hard, but also gently remind your friend of all the other hurdles that those around them are navigating. Life throws curveballs. It may not be your friend's choice to divorce, but they *can* choose *how* they divorce.

Be the wise one

You are in a unique position to help your friend navigate this well, because you aren't living the emotional roller-coaster and can help your friend to see things objectively.

When you're in the middle of the fallout from a relationship break-down, it's very tempting to think the only way through is a battle, with lawyers on each side. But adversarial litigation breeds mistrust, is hugely expensive, takes months if not years and can leave families torn apart. In fact, it's really very straightforward. At the end of the day, your friend and former partner will need a Court Order to finalize the division of their finances on divorce. And a Judge will only approve an agreement they think is objectively fair in the eyes of the law. Not what is best for one of them, but for both of them and their children.

So the sooner your friend and their former partner know what a Judge would consider fair in their situation, the sooner they can reach a fair deal knowing a Judge will endorse it. So, provided it is safe to do so, encourage your friend to view this divorce as a shared problem to be navigated with their former partner, and to take joint advice where possible. That way they can divorce well, by which we mean achieve a fair outcome on the division of finances and arrangements for children without breaking the bank or triggering huge amounts of conflict. Then they can move on.

Look to the future

Family Judges are forward looking. They will be thinking, 'What are the needs of these two adults and any children going forwards?' Encouraging your friend to look to the future is therefore a brilliant and very helpful strategy. No, the divorce may not have been their choice, but they now have the opportunity to reframe their lives and redefine themselves. This can be fun and exciting! And where a good, supportive friendship group can come into its own.

OVER TO YOU ...

'What can I say?'

It's hard to know how you come across and to reflect back on your own behaviour, especially in terms of being supportive through a divorce. We've both been in your position many times, and even knowing everything we do about divorce, good and bad, it's still so easy to say the wrong thing.

So here are some examples of the good and the bad. Read them. And the next time you're with your friend, check yourself. If you're going down the negative route, take a breath and try another way.

What *not* to stay	Try instead
I can't believe he's done this to you!	Gosh, you're going through a tough time. Let's talk about it.
I never thought she was right for you.	I guess the relationship really wasn't working for you any more. You so deserve to find happiness.
What do you mean he wants the children to stay midweek? He was always working when you were married!	It must be so hard to navigate these decisions. How are you feeling about being co-parents? You're going to need to work together on this for years – have you thought about maybe getting some professional support?
You should definitely get the house.	I've no idea what the right legal outcome is – I guess it depends massively on your own situation. You both obviously feel very differently about this – maybe some impartial legal advice would help, so you both know where you stand? You could even go together.
Divorce is hell. I'm devastated you're going through it.	I think this could be the start of something amazing for you. I heard that nearly half of all marriages end in divorce, so it's tough, but also quite normal. Let me know how I can support you.
Well, that's the last time he sets foot in my home.	I was thinking it would be good, if possible, to stay friends with both of you. Our children are so close and I think it might make it easier for them too. Let me know what you think.
Take her to the cleaners	Have you guys sat down with a financial adviser yet? I'd imagine the sooner you both understand what the finances look like, the sooner you can work out what might be fair.

I'm not surprised little Freddy doesn't want to see him. Why should he be forced to?	Wow, sounds as though Freddy is really struggling. That must be so hard. Have you thought about going to see a co-parenting expert together? Might really help Freddy.
Such a shame you can't come to the dinner party – it's just for couples.	Just no!

STEP 10

||||||||||||||||||||||||||||||||||||||||||||||||||||||||||||||||||||||||||||||||||

MAKING OUR RESHAPED FAMILY A LIFELONG REALITY

||||||||||||||||||||||||||||||||||||||||||||||||||||||||||||||||||||||||||||||||||

Addressing the key pinch points

You've made it to the final step. Well done! And this, in many ways, is the big one. Because navigating the divorce process in a fair and dignified way is a challenge which is finite. But taking that learning into your future life is a constant. Remember this is an emotional journey. The 'end' of the divorce process can in fact trigger a range of complex and sometimes confusing emotions: relief, yes, but also sadness, aimlessness, loneliness, joy. Know that it's not a straight line and work through your own emotions at your own pace. Get professional support (*back to* Step 3), if you need it. All we would like you to do is take the lessons you have picked up in this book and take them forward.

We hope you have found some helpful practical, emotional and legal pointers. You may be making progress towards a resolution of some or all of the issues that are confronting you and your family, or at the very least have a deeper understanding of what they are. Or you may only be at the stage of realizing the extent of the task in front of you, and feel daunted and slightly overwhelmed. You'll get where you want to go, don't worry.

But however far along you are, you aren't at the end. The one certainty is that your future family life, particularly if you have children, will have bumps in the road, as everyone's does. No one has all the answers, no one can anticipate everything that can and will go wrong. This step is about locking in whatever progress you've made, developing trust and resilience for the future and preparing for those bumps when they come.

Perhaps it's helpful to think of a car heading down a country track. It needs suspension. Potholes and bumps in the road are inevitable. But if you've built the car right, you can absorb the jolt, the impact, and keep going. If you haven't, you'll be in for an uncomfortable ride. Damage may result.

And in life, just as on a country road, there's no way of knowing when obstacles will appear. Some families work well together for years before issues suddenly arise out of nowhere. Perhaps someone loses their job and can't pay spousal maintenance, for example, which threatens to upset the whole financial applecart. Or one of you is offered a great job overseas.

So this step isn't about agreeing a set of rules in advance so you can read from a script when the going gets tough. It is more about developing a mindset that recognizes the ongoing nature of your commitment.

You just have to … keep going. Much of what we've had to say so far in this book could be summarized as: 'Start as you mean to continue.' But, equally, you have to 'continue as you meant to start', by which we mean that the hard work isn't over just because you've sorted the finances and/or arrangements for the children. To flog the overused car analogy to death, your ongoing relationship, like any other, will require maintenance. And kindness.

No one said it would be easy. Things *will* get easier over time, but you can't afford to take for granted the progress you've made.

COMMON PITFALLS

What we see time and again with divorcing couples is that a post-separation relationship is fragile. It can easily be derailed by life events. And life is full of changes. So what we want to do here is prepare you for the ones we see arising most often, and give you strategies for how to navigate them.

You won't know how you feel about developments like these until they happen, but identifying the issues in advance will at least prepare you to deal with them should they turn up. Here are some of the main ones:

New relationships

An early test of resolve often comes when one or other, or perhaps both, of you enter new relationships, particularly where children are involved. But accepting that each of you has the right to be happy means accepting the consequences too.

Inevitably, questions can arise to which the answers are not yet known by anyone. Where is this new relationship going? Is it 'serious'? Are you planning to live together? There will be uncertainty. And that's before the emotional impact of seeing a former partner move on. Very few of us are 'completely fine' about it, whatever we like to say.

And – often overlooked – it probably won't be straightforward for the new partner either. Walking into a functional co-parenting relationship can make them feel like a spare wheel (sorry) at times. However sensitively you approach it, it will take time for them to understand your dynamics and history, and for you to be confident that they do.

Moreover, the new partner might have their own co-parenting relationship to add into the mix, deserving of equal respect and tolerance. You may be as much a change to them and their children's family life as they are to yours. There are a lot of moving parts here. Trust, understanding and patience will be required on all sides.

As ever, communication will be key. And that has to start with the adults. As a starting-point, can you and your former partner agree that if you develop a serious relationship, you will let each other know? And that you will do so well in advance of your children knowing about it? One of the biggest triggers for conflict can be children rushing home to a co-parent to announce they have met a new boyfriend/girlfriend that that co-parent knew nothing about. Be respectful. Of course it's going to be awkward! But if you can introduce this new person to your children as someone accepted by you both, think how much easier it's going to be for you all to manage.

If you're struggling, don't forget to access expert help. You haven't been in this situation before and there's no reason to face it alone. It's normal to find this hard.

And as always, if you can, work together.

School

If you have children, their school should be a place of complete neutrality. Too often we see divorces where one parent has tried to 'get the school on side' by sharing their own perspective or narrative about the divorce. All this does is put the school in a hugely uncomfortable position and antagonize the other parent. Remember, too, that children pick up on more than you realize. The last thing they need, in this time of flux, is second-guessing what they can say to their teachers in case it gets back to the wrong parent.

So, set ground rules from Day One. Agree a joint, neutral email which you send to the school together, informing them of the divorce and asking them to keep you both apprised if your child raises any issues about it at school. Ensure you are both on all the mailing lists.

Maintain this neutral messaging where you can with the other parents. Remember that you will move on after this divorce. As we've already discussed, it won't help you to do so if everyone at the school gate is talking about your private life. So don't over-share. Remember that school is the place for your children to get support, not you. If you need impartial support, access help from someone who has the right expertise and is far removed from your children's day-to-day life. That will help them and you.

Relocations

Life moves on. What if one of you wants to move away, impacting your settled arrangements for the children? This is a relatively common issue, particularly for international families involving parents of different nationality where, say, one of them wishes to 'move back home' to be with friends and family. Indeed, these relocations can be amongst the very hardest situations known to family law: 'I have heard them described as cases which pose a dilemma rather than a problem. A problem can be solved: a dilemma is insoluble …'[1]

Sometimes there is just no pleasing everyone. Let's go back to Jan and Mick:

||||||||||||||||||||||||||||||||||||||||||||||||||||||||||||||||||||||||||||||||||||||||||||||||||||||||||

JAN AND MICK

||||||||||||||||||||||||||||||||||||||||||||||||||||||||||||||||||||||||||||||||||||||||||||||||||||||||||

Remember this family from Step 7? Imagine that, instead of becoming embroiled in highly acrimonious Court proceedings, Jan and Mick instead took early joint advice leading to an amicable separation, several years ago now.

Back then, Mick moved out of the family home to a property nearby. Not so close that he and Jan were under each other's feet, say a 25-minute drive away. Their daughter, Lucy, didn't have to move schools, which they were both pleased about.

With the building blocks in place, Jan and Mick managed to agree arrangements for Lucy without difficulty: a form of shared care where she spent each Wednesday overnight and alternate weekends with Mick during term time, and the rest with Jan, and holidays were split equally. The arrangements have worked well ever since. Lucy feels she has two homes, and Jan and Mick each have a close relationship with the school, where Lucy is progressing well.

Two years ago, Jan began a new relationship with Keith. He has now moved in with her. Mick is fine about it; he has had a number of recent short-term relationships himself. Lucy gets on well with Keith.

Out of the blue, though, Keith's employer has offered him an opportunity to work for the firm in Germany. It's more money, good for his career and he wants to take it. Jan agrees he should take it and thinks it would be a great opportunity for her and Lucy too. Jan's employer has an office in Germany, so she can easily relocate. But she is worried about Mick's reaction ...

Legally, because Mick has parental responsibility for Lucy, Jan cannot take her to live in Germany without his consent (or a Court Order). She feels caught between a rock and a hard place: Keith and Jan's employers want an answer, so Jan is under pressure to decide what she wants to do and let Keith know, but how should she approach the issue with Mick? Both of them have worked extremely hard to keep things on an even keel since they separated, and each has supported the other when they've needed it, but this is a whole new situation.

Handled wrongly, Mick is going to feel marginalized. He wonders how Jan can be suggesting this? Has she ever really respected his role as Lucy's father? He believes the priority has to be maintaining the proven arrangements for Lucy rather than prioritizing Keith's career.

From Jan's perspective, it's not up to Mick where she chooses to live. She has a right to be happy and is excited about an adventure in another country. She thinks Lucy will be too. Anyway, Germany's not that far – Mick can come out whenever he likes.

The potential to get this wrong is all too apparent. It has to be acknowledged at the outset that it isn't an easy situation for anyone – just expecting Mick to accept the plans may be as unlikely as Jan abandoning them. And Mick and Jan are only wrestling with a potential move to Germany. What if it were Sydney, or Seattle? Not that similar issues won't arise with a move closer to home, from Nottingham to Manchester perhaps, or Bristol to London. Any move that isn't right next door is going to pose a challenge to the existing arrangements.

What would the practical arrangements be in this case? Could, for example, there be an agreement for most of the holidays to be spent in England with Mick, if term time is to be spent in Germany? Would Lucy be happy with that? Is the disruption of the move worth it?

These are difficult questions about which reasonable people can disagree. Obviously, open dialogue is at an absolute premium here.

If you find yourself in a co-parenting situation where one of you is wanting to move far away, then as much as anything else it's an issue about trust. Do you trust the relocating parent to ensure your relationship with your child is prioritized following a move? If you don't, that is obviously going to be a major problem.

If you get stuck, consider what expert help you can draw on (*consider again the experts identified in* Step 3). Work together.

'What kind of parent do I need to be?'

Another common bump in the road is that your roles as parents will change over time. Once your focus may not have stretched far beyond keeping your children safe and healthy. But as they grow and become more independent, you'll probably find the emphasis switches to less immediate concerns – personal and social development, for example, or educational attainment.

The point is the dynamics of your co-parenting relationship will evolve, depending on the task at hand. This can be hard for a parent used to 'calling the shots'. But the reality, as Family Court Judges never tire of reminding us, is that we all have different strengths and weaknesses as parents, just as we do as individuals and in the end your children will benefit from the qualities each of their parents brings to the table. They will take what they need from each of you.

Setting appropriate boundaries

Which is not to say that there shouldn't be some common ground rules … At the risk of stating the obvious, older children will benefit from some consistency of approach between households. Any parent of an adolescent child will be familiar with the 'But Dad said I could stay up until 2 a.m. playing video games' line of attack. Being on the same page is obviously crucial, which in turn requires open lines of communication.

Here are some areas that can be up for discussion. Maybe none are relevant for you right now, but they probably will be at some point. Mutual recognition that these issues are coming down the track should make the business of discussing them easier when the time comes.

Homework/study out of school
- 'What are our common expectations?'
- 'If our child needs help, which of us can best provide it?'

Screen time/gaming
- 'Is this an issue for us, and if so, what restrictions should we impose?'

Social media and internet safety
- 'Do we agree to have appropriate internet controls in each of our homes and ensure they are activated?'
- 'Should we agree to monitor our child's social media, if possible?'

Body image and identity

- 'Are we creating an environment in which our child feels comfortable to express their views? If not, can we agree to get professional assistance to do so?'
- 'How can we best help our child to make the right decisions?'

Staying up late

- 'Can we agree bedtimes?'

Age-appropriate media

- 'What are we happy with our child watching/listening to?'
- 'Have appropriate content controls been activated?'

Drugs and alcohol

- 'What information do we give our child and when?'
- 'Can we provide a consistent message about what is and isn't acceptable?'

Sexuality and relationships

- 'How can we best support our child in making the right decisions about relationships, sex and sexual health?'

Finances

Hopefully you have settled, or will settle, your finances, but it's as well to bear in mind that no financial deal can completely predict the future. Any settlement is always based on a snapshot of your financial circumstances at the time, including your best guess as to what they might be in due course. But sometimes life drags us in a different direction altogether.

As we saw in Step 8, the Family Court will always try to end your financial ties to each other if it can (the so-called 'clean break'). But sometimes this is just not feasible, for example where the Court makes an order that one of you pays a monthly sum to the other. Spousal maintenance orders such as this are, in their nature, variable. This means that in the future a Court can change the amount to be paid (up or down), or can cancel the payment altogether or even capitalize it, if it considers it would be fair to do so.[2]

There may be a number of reasons why one of you considers an existing maintenance order should be changed. For example:

- The maintenance payer loses their job and can't afford it.
- The maintenance payee (i.e. the receiver of maintenance) no longer needs it.
- The maintenance payee has started living with someone who is in a position to contribute to their shared outgoings.
- The maintenance payee can't manage on the sums currently ordered and needs more.
- Either the payer or the payee wishes to discharge the monthly award by payment of a lump sum instead.

Some of these are matters of choice and others of necessity. If you lose your job, it is obvious that your ability to pay maintenance is going to be hampered, unless you have other resources. And it's not just a theoretical possibility – people *do* lose their jobs all the time. In a case where money is tight, a prolonged period of unemployment can be disastrous for both households.

The temptation is to dig in and protect your own position: 'It's not my fault, it's up to them to get a new job.' But is this reasonable? Such an approach risks pitching you into an oppositional situation, with the possibility of acrimonious Court proceedings to follow. You are risking all the hard work you have done because you have forgotten that this is a shared problem. As ever, work together if you can.

And that most likely means putting together a new budget. What are each of your immediate monthly needs, scaled back to exclude the optional extras? What sources of income do you have? Can you draw on savings in the short term? Are there other income streams which could be made available? Could family or friends help? If there is only a finite amount of money to go around, work together to make a plan which distributes it fairly between you. Now, more than ever, you really don't want to be spending money on legal fees unless there is no other way through.

Dealing with friends and family

We've already looked in Step 9 at the special responsibility your friends and family have to support you through your separation and divorce. You have to make it as easy as you can for them to support you into the future. How you communicate about your divorce and your former partner will go a long way to determining their response. If they see a generous-spirited, constructive approach from you, they are unlikely to diverge from it. You set the tone.

Needless to say, this is also what your children need to see from you.

What about your former in-laws? They are your children's grand-parents, after all. Your former partner's siblings are their aunts and uncles. Whatever the difficulties of your separation, your children need to be given emotional permission for their relationships with these people to develop and thrive. They are a fundamental part of their identity and that isn't going to change. You have to accept that and live with it as best you can.

Dealing with work

Navigating divorce, even when you are working together, is demand-ing. Which means, unsurprisingly, that divorce can have a big impact on how you perform at work. As you may recall from Step 2, a study by the *Nashville Business Journal* found that in the 6 months leading up to and the year of divorce, the divorcing employee's productivity was reduced by 40 per cent. Their productivity then suffered on some level for 5 years after the divorce.[3] Perhaps surprisingly, it also impacted the productivity of those who worked alongside them: in the 6 months leading up to and the year of a divorce, the study showed the productivity of the divorcing employee's co-workers was reduced by 4 per cent across the board.[4]

A YouGov poll featured in *The Sunday Times* which interviewed 500 high-earners (with annual salaries ranging from £100k to multi-million pound packages) painted a worrying picture:

- Of those interviewed, 69 per cent admitted 'significant' problems in their relationships in their current or similar role (compared with the national average of 20 per cent).
- One quote from an employee really summed up the issue: '*I get the sense that most employers believe you should leave all home problems at home. Yet employers expect work to be able to intrude on your home life. This has to be a two-way street.*'[5]

This comes back to where we began: the stigma surrounding divorce. Many employers just haven't wanted to go there, anxious they may become embroiled in an adversarial process they'd rather avoid. Again, this speaks to the need for us all to change the way we view divorce. In the same way that employers have a bereavement policy, they should also have a divorce or family change policy.

But back to the here and now – what can you do? It obviously depends on your relationship with your employer, but it can help to communicate what is happening. There is no need for any details, but just the headline that you are getting divorced, working together amicably, but clearly there may be occasions when you need to take some time off to work through the practicalities and access legal and financial advice. Then try, if you can, to hold back on any further discussion with your co-workers. As we've already discussed, it won't help you if your divorce becomes the topic of conversation around the water cooler. Let work be the place you go to switch off from the issues you are navigating in your personal life. And when it's clear that you need some time away from the office, try to take it.

If you are in a managerial role, do consider what you as an employer could do better in the future. Could you develop a family change policy entitling your employees to a certain number of days off to navigate their separation? Do you have an existing wellness programme? Many employers offer annual presentations for employees on various wellness initiatives; alongside talks on self-care and managing stress, there should be sections on how to approach divorce well and how to co-parent well following divorce and separation.

At the very least, be mindful of divorce in the workspace. The likelihood is you are not alone, that others are going through it right now too. And know that it is normal that divorce will impact work. So all the more reason, if you can, to work through it together, so you get to the other side with the minimum possible stress.

LOVE CAN ENDURE

This may not be the right mindset for your situation. But for some separating couples, the idea of love enduring divorce can be very comforting. If you feel like it, it may be worth letting it settle in your subconscious.

> Love is patient, love is kind, it is not envious. Love does not brag, it is not puffed up. It is not rude, it is not self-serving, it is not easily angered or resentful. It is not glad about injustice, but rejoices in the truth. It bears all things, believes all things, hopes all things, endures all things.
>
> 1 Corinthians 13:8

We often talk of love surviving death. Why then, can't love, in some form, survive divorce?

This can be overwhelming at first to process, so start modestly. If you have children with your former spouse, you'll know your love for your children endures. And when we spoke about co-parenting in

Steps 5 and 7, you'll have seen that for most families the best way to care for the children is to care for the co-parent. So the love you feel for the parenting role they play in your child's life can endure.

Take this as a starting-point and then, if you can, go deeper. There was once so much love between you. Can it be retained, or some of it retained, in a different form? Can you commit to being there for each other, not simply as co-parents but also as friends? This is an emotional journey and you may need support with it. Don't be afraid to get a counsellor or therapist involved. Where can you go from here? Can you acknowledge that your past love is greater than your present divorce? Keep talking, respect each other and respect the love you once had for each other and you may discover new emotional territory.

You

Finally, don't forget about yourself ... Overlaying everything else, there is a subtle piece of work that needs doing that is nothing to do with the practicalities at all: who are *you* going to be, now that you're moving on from being part of this couple? What are you moving on to?

You can't unlive the experiences of your time in this partnership, and why would you want to? As we've attempted to argue throughout this book, just because your relationship has run its course doesn't mean it has failed, or even that it is regrettable. This is obvious if you have children together, but is equally valid if you don't. You can't erase the past. It will always be with you. But you can move forward into a future of your choosing.

Of course, separating *is* a reassertion of your own identity to some extent: of your individuality, living outside the role that you assumed and became accustomed to within your relationship. The Japanese symbolize this with the ritual smashing of wedding rings with a large hammer. 'Divorce parties' may fulfil a similar need for some. No doubt there is a catharsis in there somewhere. Whatever gets you through. But the reality is that if you intend to have a positive future relationship with your former partner then you will need to allow yourself to feel good about what came beforehand. Recognize what you both did right in your relationship. Celebrate those things and keep them close. The rest you can discard.

Finally, take a moment to congratulate yourself

The fact that you are reading this book shows you have the motivation to divorce well. You have the strength of character to push back on the negative stereotypes and find a better way for your family to navigate this life change. Nothing about working together is easy. There will be bumps in the road. But the stakes are high for you and your family. What we want to do, more than anything else, is motivate you to believe that a 'good divorce' is achievable. And to open your eyes to how unappealing, and damaging, the alternatives can be.

We have seen all kinds of families arguing about all manner of issues, from the trivial to the profound. We mean no disrespect to any of them by saying that the great majority of these cases represent a failure: of a legal system uniquely unsuited to the demands of separating families and of a wider culture prone to a horribly misanthropic view of divorce. Changing this requires a mindset reboot.

We all have our parts to play in achieving this. As separating individuals, we have to stay focused on what is really important and what isn't. As friends and family watching from the sidelines, we have to make sure we aren't adding to the problem, however worthy our intentions. As employers, we have to recognize the extent of this life change and do better at providing support. And as professionals working in this field, lawyers and non-lawyers alike, we have to be mindful of how we can best support our clients, even if this means referring them to services we don't ourselves offer. Working together applies to the professionals as much as anyone else.

And as a final reminder, consider the following selection of excerpts from cases to give you a flavour of what family disputes actually look like in reality, once you reach the Family Court. Of course these are just words on a page – we can't adequately convey the experience of actually participating as a litigant. But even so …

Crowther v Crowther [2021]

There appears to have been an almost complete breakdown of constructive communication … Each party thinks the other is, to use their own words, 'out to destroy' them … I asked myself on a number of occasions whether the aggressive approach adopted by each side has achieved anything; it seems to me that it has led to vast costs and reduced scope for settlement. The toll on each party is incalculable (W was visibly distressed during the hearing) and, from what I have heard, the impact on the children has been highly detrimental.

JM v KK [2021]

This case has been a classic example of how what is sometimes described as small money cases can be infinitely more difficult than cases involving larger sums. It is impossible to find a solution that can leave both parties happy. The decisions that each party took as the marriage broke down and in their understandable desire to be the carer of their daughter have been hugely detrimental financially to them both.

OG v AG [2020]

It is important that I enunciate this principle loud and clear: if, once the financial landscape is clear, you do not openly negotiate reasonably, then you will likely suffer a penalty in costs. This applies whether the case is big or small, or whether it is being decided by reference to needs or sharing.

T v T [2010]

> [The parents] must put aside their differences ... if the adults do not manage to resolve things by communicating with each other, the children inevitably suffer and the adults may also pay the price when the children are old enough to be aware of what has been going on ... It is a tremendous privilege to be involved in bringing up a child. Childhood is over all too quickly and, whilst I appreciate that both sides think that they are motivated only by concern for the children, it is still very sad to see it being allowed to slip away whilst energy is devoted to adult wrangles and to litigation. What is particularly unfair is that the legacy of a childhood tainted in that way is likely to remain with the children into their own adult lives.

So, from us to you, may you choose the divorce that is right for you and your family. And hopefully never become the name on a case report. Know that the challenges of working together pale into insignificance compared to the stress of working against each other.

OVER TO YOU ...

Reflections

You've made it to the end. Now is the time to return to your Step 1 goals, find a quiet moment to sit down with a cup of coffee and reflect on where you've got to. How successful do you think you have been?

It can be hard to remain goal-focused when you're absorbed in the granular detail of budgets or legal principle, or if you've found reaching agreement more difficult than you were hoping. So take a piece of paper and note down where you've got to and what more needs to be done. Perhaps you've developed your thinking as time has progressed and you've identified new priorities. But don't be tempted to stray too far from what you both thought was important at the outset; the big picture stuff is unlikely to have changed very much.

And it's those big picture themes that will ground you when you're running off-course. So take out your goals and reflect on them, together or apart, and remember that wherever you are in the process, you're doing great.

Notes and References

Internet addresses (websites, blogs, etc.) printed in this book are offered as a resource to you. These are not intended in any way to be or imply an endorsement on the part of HarperCollins, nor do we vouch for the content of these sites and numbers for the life of this book. Though correct at the time of finalising the book for publication, this information can change and is beyond the publishers' control.

Prologue

1. https://webarchive.nationalarchives.gov.uk/ukgwa/20160106011951/
http://www.ons.gov.uk/ons/rel/vsob1/divorces-in-england-and-wales/2011/sty-what-percentage-of-marriages-end-in-divorce.html

Step 1: Setting Our Goals

1. https://www.pewresearch.org/social-trends/2013/06/13/chapter-4-marriage-and-parenting/#reasons-for-getting-married
2. https://www.wired.co.uk/article/what-is-love
3. https://www.ons.gov.uk/peoplepopulationandcommunity/birthsdeathsandmarriages/divorce
4. https://www.bbc.com/future/article/20200313-how-your-personality-changes-as-you-age
5. https://www.difi.org.qa/wp-content/uploads/2017/11/Ignacio_Socias.pdf

6. https://www.ons.gov.uk/peoplepopulationandcommunity/birthsdeaths andmarriages/divore/bulletins/divorcesenglandandwales/2019

7. https://ideas.ted.com/pride-can-be-a-virtue-but-it-needs-to-be-the-right-kind-of-pride/

8. Ibid.

9. Ibid.

10. https://www.qualitative-research.net/index.php/fqs/article/view/66/135

11. https://www.psychologistworld.com/influence/social-influence

12. Asch, S. E., and Guetzkow, H. (1951). 'Effects of group pressure upon the modification and distortion of judgments', *Groups, Leadership, and Men*, 222–236

Step 2: Agreeing Our Plan of Action

1. Under the Children Act 1989

2. Under the Matrimonial Causes Act 1973

3. Sir James Munby, 'Unheard Voices: The involvement of children and vulnerable people in the family justice system', *Family Law* 45(8): 895–902

4. https://www.judiciary.uk/wp-content/uploads/2020/11/FamilySolutions GroupReport_WhatAboutMe_12November2020.pdf-final.pdf

5. Ibid.

6. Sir Andrew McFarlane, keynote address to the Resolution conference, 5 April 2019

7. https://resolution.org.uk/wp-content/uploads/2021/05/Resolution-Wellbeing-Report-FINAL.pdf

8. https://www.wellbeingatthebar.org.uk/problems/vicarious-trauma

9. https://www.judiciary.uk/wp-content/uploads/2020/11/FamilySolutions GroupReport_WhatAboutMe_12November2020.pdf-final.pdf

10. His Honour Judge Wildblood, in a case called Re B, [2020]

11. https://www.lawgazette.co.uk/news/parents-could-face-costs-order-for-clogging-up-family-Court/5110452.article

12. www.qredible.co.uk/b/how-many-marriages-end-in-divorce

13. Mr Justice Holman, *Luckwell v Limata* [2014]

14. Bentham, quoted ibid.
15. https://www.judiciary.uk/wp-content/uploads/2021/10/Confidence-and-Confidentiality-Transparency-in-the-Family-Courts-final.pdf
16. By Rayden solicitors.
17. https://www.bizjournals.com/nashville/blog/2014/03/the-cost-of-divorce-to-employers.html
18. 'What could a public health approach to family justice look like?', The Nuffield Foundation, 2019
19. Harold, G., Acquah, D., Sellers, R., and Chowdry, H. (2016), 'What works to enhance inter-parental relationships and improve outcomes for children', Department of Work and Pensions
20. https://www.gov.uk/guidance/reducing-parental-conflict-the-impact-on-children
21. Seddons.
22. www.moneyadviceservice.org.uk
23. See Aviva's 2018 'Family Finances Report'.

Step 3: Deciding What Professional Support We Need

1. https://www.nuffieldfoundation.org/sites/default/files/files/Guide_To_The_Treatment_of_Pensions_on_Divorce-Digital(1).pdf
2. The Pensions Advisory Group, 'A Guide to the Treatment of Pensions on Divorce', July 2019
3. https://www.aviva.com/newsroom/news-releases/2018/01/cost-of-divorce-and-separation-surpasses-14500-pounds-for-uk-couples/
4. https://resolution.org.uk/
5. https://www.barstandardsboard.org.uk/resources/public-access-guidance-for-lay-clients.html
6. In our experience, most couples, even when they are agreed, want to know for their own reassurance that it is a legally fair agreement which they won't come to regret in future.
7. https://www.judiciary.uk/wp-content/uploads/2020/11/FamilySolutionsGroupReport_WhatAboutMe_12November2020-2.pdf-final-2.pdf

Step 4: Making Short-Term Plans

1. You would be committing the criminal offence of bigamy, under the Offences Against the Person Act 1857.
2. https://www.gov.uk/government/news/divorce-blame-game-to-end
3. Owens v Owens [2018]
4. British Social Attitudes 36, 2019 edition
5. https://www.ons.gov.uk/peoplepopulationandcommunity/ birthsdeathsandmarriages/families/datasets/ familiesandhouseholdsfamiliesandhouseholds
6. As a general rule, child maintenance is not dealt with by the Courts but by the Child Maintenance Service.
7. S.3(1) Children Act 1989
8. https://www.gov.uk/apply-council-tax-reduction
9. https:www.gov.uk/benefits-calculators

Step 5: Starting to Talk about the Children

1. A number of resources for those suffering from domestic abuse are listed at: https://www.gov.uk/guidance/domestic-abuse-how-to-get-help.
2. https://www.nationalinterest.org/blog/buzz/scientist-explained-us-humans-are-hardwired-love-each-other-123581
3. https://www.familymediationcouncil.org.uk/wp-content/uploads/ 2019/09/Top-Tips-for-parents-FJYPB.pdf and https://www.cafcass.gov. uk/family-justice-young-peoples-board/
4. https://www.nuffieldfjo.org.uk/wp-content/uploads/2021/05/What-could-a-public-health-approach-to-family-justice-look-like.pdf
5. https://www.difi.org.qa/wp-content/uploads/2017/11/Ignacio_ Socias.pdf
6. https://www.cafcass.gov.uk/grown-ups/parents-and-carers/divorce-and-separation/parenting-together/parenting-plan

Step 6: Building Our Financial Picture

1. https://www.nuffieldfoundation.org/sites/default/files/files/Guide_To_The_Treatment_of_Pensions_on_Divorce-Digital(1).pdf
2. https://assets.publishing.service.gov.uk/government/uploads/system/uploads/attachment_data/file/953463/form-e-eng.pdf
3. https://www.research.manchester.ac.uk/portal/en/publications/pensions-and-divorce-exploratory-analysis-of-quantitative-data(b4cadc0b-d6db-4e57-919e-a6af03e4ad47).html
4. The Pensions Advisory Group, 'A Guide to the Treatment of Pensions on Divorce', July 2019
5. https://www.tax.service.gov.uk/calculate-stamp-duty-land-tax/#/intro
6. https://assets.publishing.service.gov.uk/government/uploads/system/uploads/attachment_data/file/951188/form-e1-eng.pdf

Step 7: Reaching a Co-Parenting Agreement

1. Re G (Children) [2006] 2 FLR 629, HL
2. Section 13 of the Children Act 1989
3. https://assets.publishing.service.gov.uk/government/uploads/system/uploads/attachment_data/file/895173/assessing-risk-harm-children-parents-pl-childrens-cases-report_.pdf
4. https://www.cafcass.gov.uk/grown-ups/professionals/ciaf/
5. CIAF glossary of terms downloaded from https://www.cafcass.gov.uk/grown-ups/professionals/ciaf/
6. If you're interested, the broad framework is set out in the following flowchart: https://www.justice.gov.uk/downloads/family-justice-reform/cap-flowchart.pdf
7. https://www.cafcass.gov.uk/grown-ups/parents-and-carers/divorce-and-separation/parenting-together/separated-parents-information-programme/#:~:text=The%20Separated%20Parents%20Information%20Programme%20%28SPIP%29%20%20a,dispute%20with%20your%20child%E2%80%99s%20other%20parent%20or%20carer
8. Re F (A Child) (International Relocation Cases) [2017] 1 FLR 979, CA

9. CIAF glossary of terms downloaded from https://www.cafcass.gov.uk/grown-ups/professionals/ciaf/

10. https://www.judiciary.uk/wp-content/uploads/2018/06/speech-lj-mcfarlane-fnf.pdf

Step 8: Reaching a Financial Agreement

1. https://bills.parliament.uk/publications/42276/documents/566. Amongst other things, the Bill proposes to restrict claims to spousal maintenance to terms of no longer than 5 years 'unless the Court is satisfied that there is no other means of making provision for a party to the marriage and that that party would otherwise be likely to suffer serious financial hardship as a result'.

2. The payment of cash lump sums was introduced in 1963 and transfers of property in 1971.

3. S.25(1) Matrimonial Causes Act 1973

4. S.25A(1)

5. S.25A(2)

6. In accordance with the Law Commission's influential 2014 report 'Matrimonial Property, Needs and Agreements'; http://www.lawcom.gov.uk/app/uploads/2015/03/lc343_matrimonial_property.pdf

7. *Wachtel v Wachtel* [1973]

Step 9: Managing Our Friends and Family

1. https://www.ons.gov.uk/peoplepopulationandcommunity/births deathsandmarriages/divorce/bulletins/divorcesinenglandandwales/2012-12-20

2. https://www.ons.gov.uk/peoplepopulationandcommunity/birthsdeathsandmarriages/divorce

3. https://www.nuffieldfjo.org.uk/wp-content/uploads/2021/05/What-could-a-public-health-approach-to-family-justice-look-like.pdf

4. https://4bc.co.uk/wp-content/uploads/2019/08/FLBA_FA72_online_WBandBigC.pdf

5. https://www.wsj.com/articles/tired-of-being-told-cheer-up-the-problem-of-toxic-positivity-11635858001

6. Quoted ibid.

Step 10: Making Our Reshaped Family a Lifelong Reality

1. Diana Bryant, Australian jurist and Chief Justice of the Family Court of Australia, 2004–17

2. S.31 of the Matrimonial Causes Act 1973

3. https://www.bizjournals.com/nashville/blog/2014/03/the-cost-of-divorce-to-employers.html

4. Ibid.

5. https://www.thetimes.co.uk/article/high-flyers-pay-a-price-in-misery-at-home-ggctmcb68

Afterword
and Thanks

This is not the first book we have *tried* to write together. A previous one hoped to cast light on a very complicated aspect of the law to do with the international enforcement of maintenance orders. After months of on-and-off endeavour, we came up with something unreadably turgid. Then we realized we'd completely failed to consider the impact of an absolutely central piece of legislation we'd never heard of. It was a relief to give up!

With this book, we realize that we run the risk of annoying every specialist in this area: not enough law for the lawyers, too much for everyone else. But this is a practical guide, not a textbook. With the help of the indefatigable team at HarperCollins, we've tried to provide something of general help to those who need it and to spark a conversation about why divorce might need a rethink.

We owe a great deal to one man, who died some years before *The Divorce Surgery* was conceived and even more before this goes to print. His name was Lionel Swift QC and he was the best of us. A lawyer of tremendous warmth, energy and judgement, he was largely responsible (with apologies to the stellar cast who succeeded him) for the creation of our barristers' chambers at 4 Paper Buildings, now 4PB, where we both trained and qualified. Lionel showed that you don't have to be difficult or aggressive or surly or positional to be a family lawyer, and that being civilized and 'getting results' aren't mutually exclusive.

Thanks must also go to another giant of Family Law, the former President of the Family Division, Sir James Munby. His early public endorsement of *The Divorce Surgery* was a game-changer for us, and eased the constant anxiety in the early days that we were going to be tapped on the shoulder and told this ambitious plan of advising couples together was, for some reason that we had failed to grasp, simply not permitted.

Particular thanks to all our colleagues and friends at 4PB, but especially to Alex Verdan QC, Charles Hale QC, Barbara Mills QC, Cyrus Larizadeh QC, Jo Brown, Nick Fairbank, Andrew Powell and, running the show, Michael Reeves. To the team at HarperCollins, particularly Lydia Good for her patience and flexibility and to Elizabeth Henry for correcting our many errors with tact and discretion. And, of course, to David Luxton and Nick Walters at David Luxton Associates, without whom none of this would have happened. When we sent a rather tentative email in December 2020, we never thought for a second they'd be interested, let alone that there was a book deal in it.

Our sincere thanks to Saffron Griffin.

The Divorce Surgery is nothing without our amazing team. Claire, Rachel, Neil and Natalie, thank you for picking up the slack on the many occasions we went off-grid to write this. Bill, thank you so much for your invaluable contribution to Step 5, and for the magic you spin in every case we've been on together. And Nichole Farrow, thank you for your words of wisdom.

Sam

On a personal note, thank you, Nikki, for being a proofreading legend. No doubt you did it in 6 hours flat whilst drinking a G&T and listening to a podcast. My parents, friends and family, you are everything to me. Thank you for enduring all my tedious divorce chat over the years and (largely) hiding your boredom. James, Isabella and Hugo, thank you for making everything else a footnote. Let's hide under the duvet and eat peanut butter forever. And thanks to Teddy and Moose, my canine therapists. I am convinced every case would settle if you were the tribunal. Finally, thank you to my co-author, for keeping our promise that this would never feel like a job. It still doesn't.

Harry

To Alice, Cecily, Walter and Nell, thank you for indulging my authorial pretensions. You have made writing this actually enjoyable, for me at least. To all those caught in the crossfire of my ramblings about this project, my apologies and thanks. To my parents, I am more grateful than I can say. Lastly to my co-author, I thought this book was a long shot, but you reduce the odds again and again.

*

And finally, from both of us, thank you to all those who've entrusted their separations to us over the years. It's always been a privilege and this book was inspired by each of you. Thank you.

Index